A Fairway to Heaven

A FAIRWAY TO HEAVEN

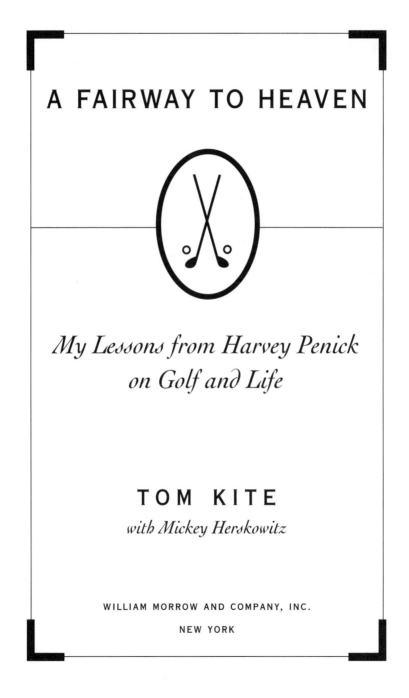

*My Lessons from Harvey Penick
on Golf and Life*

TOM KITE

with Mickey Herskowitz

WILLIAM MORROW AND COMPANY, INC.

NEW YORK

Excerpts from Harvey Penick's diary reprinted by permission of
Tinsley Penick and *Golf Digest* magazine.
Tom Kite's professional record reprinted by permission of the PGA Tour.
Unless otherwise noted, photographs are from
the collection of Tom Kite, Jr.

It is the policy of William Morrow and Company, Inc.,
and its imprints and affiliates, recognizing the importance of
preserving what has been written, to print the books we publish
on acid-free paper, and we exert our best efforts to that end.

Library of Congress Cataloging-in-Publication Data

Kite, Tom.
A fairway to heaven : my lessons from Harvey Penick on golf and
life / Tom Kite with Mickey Herskowitz.
p.   cm.
ISBN 0–688–14672–4
1. Penick, Harvey.   2. Golf coaches—United States—Biography.
3. Kite, Tom.   4. Golf.   5. Golfers—Conduct of life.
I. Herskowitz, Mickey.   II. Title.
GV964.P44F37   1997

796.352'092—dc21
[B]   97-21279
CIP

Printed in the United States of America

First Edition

1   2   3   4   5   6   7   8   9   10

BOOK DESIGN BY DEBBIE GLASSERMAN

Acknowledgments

In golf one person swings the club, and except for his caddy, the others behind a successful golfer's career often go unnoticed. I've found it is pretty much the same in publishing a book.

I am indebted to Harvey Penick's wife, Helen, and his son, Tinsley, for sharing their memories and family history, and for a lifetime of friendship.

For their research and fact checking, my thanks are owed to Dianne Reed and Dave Lancer of the PGA Tour staff; Julius Mason and the media relations office of the PGA of America, who provided timely information on the Ryder Cup; and Margaret Jamison of the *Houston Chronicle* library.

I am always thankful for the presence in my life of Christy Kite, but she needs further acknowledgment here for her help in handling requests and maintaining peace and order. I am grateful to my parents, Mauryene and Tom Kite, Sr., for their support and for putting together scrapbooks that reflect in loving detail almost every stroke of my golf career.

For their guidance, my thanks to a persevering editor, Larry Hughes, who is as passionate about golf as he is about books, and his assistant, the dedicated Patricia Ford, for her excellent line editing and photo research.

And a final thanks to Bob Rotella and my friends at the Austin Country Club for their encouragement.

To my wife, Christy,
our daughter, Stephanie,
and our sons, David and
Paul—my grand slam.

Contents

A Fairway to Heaven

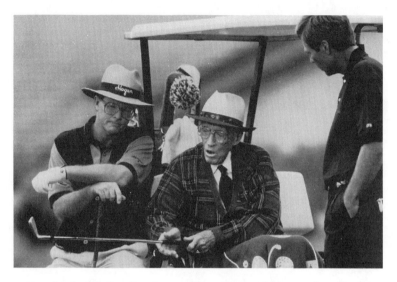

A teacher for life: Ben Crenshaw and I never stopped learning from Harvey. This particular lesson was filmed for an NBC-TV special on Harvey Penick at the Austin Country Club in February 1994. Gary Edwards

Chapter One

A TEACHER FOR
A LIFETIME

I believe it is safe to say that not many people are big fans of the Internal Revenue Service. But I owe everything to the IRS. Well, maybe not everything—more like 38 percent and a sincere thank-you.

My father, Tom, Sr., had a career in the civil service with the IRS, and in 1973 the agency transferred him from its office in Dallas to Austin. It would take a book to describe what that move meant to me. This is that book.

A writer in Jacksonville, Florida, Chris Smith, was the one who made me recall those days. He was doing a survey of players on the tour, asking each of us about the best break we ever had in golf. Fred Couples picked that famous shot in 1992, the year he won the Masters, when his ball just hung miraculously up there on the slope at Number 12 in Augusta without rolling back into the creek. A Kodak moment. A magic minute. I knew this is what writers want. And I couldn't come up with a comparable experience.

I thought hard about it that night, and the next day I found Chris and told him, "My best break was my dad being transferred to Austin when I was thirteen years old. The reason is, I came into contact with Harvey Penick and with Ben Crenshaw, whom he was coaching at the time. In my wildest dreams, I couldn't have hoped for a finer teacher. Nor could I have found a stronger competitor—or better friend—than Ben Crenshaw." If you're trying to become a good player, that is about as good as it gets. Falling into that nest was pure luck, and from that time on fate took its course.

Fate's course happened to include the Austin Country Club, at the center of the Texas pipeline. Virtually every Texas golfer who went on the tour passed through Austin. Many others lived and grew up there, and most sought out Harvey Penick to draw on the knowledge he shared so fully. Dave Marr, Davis Love III, Terry Dill, Don Massengale, Billy Maxwell, Betsy Rawls, Kathy Whitworth, Mickey Wright, Ben Crenshaw, me . . . the list goes on and on.

By the time he was eight, Ben had been identified as

a child prodigy in Austin golfing circles. You could see even then what a fine athlete he was. Mr. Penick worried about losing him to baseball, as he had Ben's older brother, Charlie, Jr. Charlie gave up golf to play the outfield on a fine University of Texas team that went to the College World Series three times. One of his teammates was Burt Hooton, who made it to the majors and pitched for the Dodgers in three World Series.

But Ben stuck with golf. We both had dads who cut down clubs for us when we were just out of the toddler stage. Mr. Crenshaw had cut down a 7-iron for Ben and sent him to Mr. Penick. The story of their first lesson became a bit inflated over the years, as golf stories sometimes do. Mr. Penick was amused when Jim Trinkle, a respected Fort Worth writer, embellished the tale in print: "He said I pointed Ben toward the green and told him to hit it out there. He did, about a hundred yards. Then I said, 'Let's go putt it in.' And Trinkle had Ben saying, 'Why didn't you tell me that in the first place?'"

I hadn't even heard about Mr. Penick until I was almost ready to leave Dallas, where I was winning tournaments in my age group. I had been playing golf with my dad, Tom Kite, Sr., since I was three years old, when I swung a cut-down club for the first time and then fell asleep on

Me at the age of two with my parents, Mauryene and Tom, Sr., on Easter Sunday, 1952. A year later I would begin playing golf with a cut-down club. Courtesy of Tom Kite, Sr.

the Austin Country Club and decided to become a member. "You're not going to believe this," he told me, "but over there they play the ball down!" At River Lake you seldom played it down due to the condition of the course.

I may be dating myself here, but this is a term you hardly hear anymore because today even small, rural courses have drainage systems. At River Lake, the frequent flooding left the surface so mushy that shots tended to dig into the turf, and we used the "drop-and-place" rule.

I was a thirteen-year-old kid who hadn't paid much attention to anything happening outside of Dallas and who knew very little about Austin or the University of Texas. But before my family moved, I began to take an interest. I paid special attention when I heard the club members in Dallas talking about a golf teacher in Austin, who also coached the university team. They would quote him: Harvey says this and Harvey says that. But Mr. Penick still wasn't a household name, and I wasn't jumping up and down, yelling, "Boy, oh, boy, I'm going to take lessons from Harvey Penick."

I was more interested in Mr. Penick's golf course and, almost before I knew it, I was there. We made the move the summer before I started eighth grade, and a whole new world opened up to me. Now, the Austin Country Club wasn't in nearly the first-class condition that it was

a blanket while Dad continued to practice. I can't
member ever not wanting to play golf.

I took my first formal lessons from the club pro
River Lake Country Club, where we were members.
name was Joe Driesbeck and no one outworked him.
was not the caliber of teacher Mr. Penick was—nor
anyone else, for that matter—but Joe won respect as
old-style pro. That is, he took care of his members.
knew everything about them that related to their
game and their needs at the club. And he ran a ter
junior program.

You had to be eight to enter the program. Mom
Dad appealed to Joe to let me join when I was sev
He agreed—my first exemption—"as long as he pays
tention." I just flat loved it. The club had a junior
school and summer camps and a play day, the same
Ladies' Day or Doctors' Day. I took a big step right th
taking all the opportunity I needed to play. It gave
a solid base to build on.

River Lake, I ought to make clear, was not a weal
person's club. The course was hard by the Trinity R
and was subject to flooding and other problems. It
never in especially good condition when I was gr
ing up.

My dad started spending time in Austin, before
moved the family, and he came home one day fairly
cited over a discovery he had made. He had checked

With my two best friends: Harvey Penick and Ben Crenshaw
Copyright © 1983 by Jeff Rowe

later, and certainly not in the shape the new location is in now. But for the first time, I could play the ball down and the fairways were smooth.

When I finally met Mr. Penick, he seemed old to me even then. He was in his late sixties, and I was struck by his face—a great, kindly face that made me think, *This is what God must look like.* It was lined and weathered and I felt I could read the Dead Sea Scrolls in it. The wrinkles in the back of his neck were deep and crisscrossed, like a road map that had been folded over and over again. The funny thing is, and I think his wife, Helen, would agree, he looked older when I first met him than he did in his eighties. His skin tightened as he aged, and he actually lost many of his wrinkles.

But it wasn't my intention to paint a portrait of Harvey Penick. My interest was in learning how to play the best golf I possibly could, and I quickly realized that I had stumbled onto something of a gold mine. You couldn't miss the awe everybody felt for him. He offered an opportunity that I would never have had in a lot of other places.

By then I had heard so much about Harvey Penick that it wasn't long before I asked him for a lesson. When Mr. Penick gave a lesson for the first time, he would walk or ride with you up to the practice tee and on the way ask about what you were trying to accomplish. What are your goals? How have you been hitting the ball lately? Has anything about your game been troubling you? He would do this to get a little head start, and by the time the lesson began he had a pretty good feel for what was in your mind.

I remember riding up the hill with him in the cart for my first lesson, full of eagerness and full of myself. Over the years I have become aware that this kind of conviction is rare, but I was thirteen years old, and I already knew what my job was going to be. I knew that nothing was going to stand in the way of my going on the PGA Tour.

My certainty worried my mother a bit, and she tried to lower my expectations. She would pull a number out of the air and say, "Of all the fine college golfers, less than two percent ever get on the tour." And I would answer, "Well, somebody's gonna make it. Why can't it be me?"

I don't want to belabor this, but I had been to a couple of Dallas Opens where I had been motivated watching players like Palmer and Nicklaus and even Sam Snead. It all added to my determination. In my mind, playing on the tour wasn't a dream. It was a commitment.

I'm sure I inherited this drive from my dad. He just has that bulldog quality. If he starts a task, he's going to finish it. And I can't say that I needed much in the way of inspiration. I was hooked on golf the first time I ever made contact with a ball. It was like discovering candy.

As I scooted along in the cart with Mr. Penick for my lesson, I heard him say, "We need to get your game in good enough shape so you can make the junior high team." I was stunned. I turned to look at him, thinking, *Make the junior high team? I'm going to be the best player on that team. I AM the best player.* Then he said, "Of course, after junior high we want to see you make the high school team."

Mr. Penick's every word was intended to give me encouragement and reassurance, and I would come to learn over the years that he never gave you anything less. But I was a thirteen-year-old brat and flying through my brain was, *Wait a minute, he has already missed the boat. He doesn't understand how good I am or how good I'm going to be.*

Looking back, I can smile, if not quite laugh out loud, at my conceit. No one could have accused me of lacking confidence. In truth, while growing up in Dallas I had not been exposed to the number and quality of players my age that I was about to find in Austin. So when I started playing there I got knocked down a little by the competition. Slowly, I understood that Mr. Penick's trick was to keep me moving in the right direction, to get me from A to B and not skip instantly to Z, as long as I reached it eventually. Even after I was on the tour and having some success, his goal for me was to improve a little bit at a time. He would toss out one of his sayings: "If you like the medicine, it doesn't mean you should take the whole bottle." Very much a measured man in everything he did, he had more patience than any of a thousand people I knew.

He was always saying, "All I do is guide the learning." To that end, he would match the amount of time and effort you were willing to put into it with his own time, always accommodating you. He never gave me any sign or hint that he saw in me anything special. It wasn't necessary; he showed it by the amount of time he spent with me.

Having said that, I ought to add that he gave as much of himself to an average weekend golfer who was a 100 shooter and trying to get down to 90. That was just as important to him as my progress or Ben Crenshaw's.

Mr. Penick always understood that different styles or attitudes worked for different kinds of golfers. "A teaching golf pro is like a cook," he said. "He mixes it up—a little salt here, a little pepper there, where it's needed. You don't teach everyone alike." He pointed out that Ben Crenshaw, like Byron Nelson, wasn't a fanatic about practicing. They were players. "But Tommy," he would tell reporters, "is like Hogan. He practices just as much as he plays." True. I guess I became almost notorious for how long I would practice—up to nine hours a day. Bob Toski asked him once why he didn't make Ben practice more. Mr. Penick shook his head and said, "He'd just learn a new way to do the wrong thing."

Negative thoughts did not come easily to Harvey Penick, who was doling out positive reinforcement long before social workers discovered that phrase. On the other hand, he didn't find it necessary to constantly tell us how good we were. All of us can see the leader board. We can read the scores. We know when we're winning.

There were occasions, of course, when he felt he needed to bring a player back down to earth. I recall a

I will always take a pointer from the great Byron Nelson (left), and share his taste in neckties. I was honored to win the Nelson award as the tour's scoring leader in 1981 and 1982.

couple of sly reminders that I wasn't as good as I thought I was. One of these was when I was fifteen or sixteen. I was back in Austin after winning a junior tournament, and the word had got around to Mr. Penick that Tommy was acting a little "cocky."

The next time I asked him for a lesson, we went to the practice range, and he watched me hit a few shots. As we started to walk away, he said, "You've been playing well and I'm very proud of you. But I want you to remember this: You are what you are, not what you do."

There was no doubt in my mind what he meant. When I told this story for Harvey Penick's *Little Green Book (And If You Play Golf, You're My Friend)*, his second, fast-selling collection of tips and musings from a lifetime in golf, I said I have tried to live by that statement ever since. And I always will.

Mr. Penick never did any group teaching. I don't think anyone would regard golf as a form of group therapy. You can't put fifteen or thirty people together and expect them to learn. Nor did he get into comparisons. We—the kids—would compare notes, but Mr. Penick would never say, "I'm working with Ben on this and Bob on that and Lester on whatever."

His golden rule was simply, Be yourself. When I came back from watching the Dallas Open one year, I said to him, "I had a chance to follow Gary Player. He really closes up his stance. I thought I'd try that a little bit. What do you think?"

His response was, "Well-l-l, that seems to work pretty good for Gary Player, but I kind of think we should stick to being Tommy." I loved hearing those words. That was his way of saying you can admire these guys all you want, but you don't need them to be your heroes. You heard people talk of Arnold Palmer and Jack Nicklaus as gods, but Mr. Penick would never consider saying anything of that kind. He wanted you to learn from these great players, not worship them.

From the start, I was very inquisitive about most things. I always raised questions. That was my nature. But I accepted just about everything Harvey Penick said as gospel. Even now, two years after his death, there are few things I come across that would replace his theories. He believed strongly that there was room for individuality on the golf course, that not every swing needed to look like every other swing. He didn't want to clone you.

Mr. Penick never had any problem with my talking to other teachers; in fact, he encouraged it. When I first went on tour, he told me that if I got into any trouble with my game and I was on the East Coast, to be sure and call Davis Love, Jr. At the time, Davis was teaching at the Atlanta Country Club (later he went to Sea Island, Georgia). He was teaching Mr. Penick's game.

Davis had played for Mr. Penick at the University of Texas and had picked up many ideas from him. He even took his mild-mannered approach to teaching as well as his philosophy.

The concept Harvey Penick taught was really quite simple. Your swing is the game. And the golf swing is nothing less than pure physics. You put the clubface against the ball at a certain rate of speed, and at a certain face angle, and it will produce a certain trajectory—the characteristic of a shot.

Mr. Penick always stressed alignment. He would set down a club in between the ball and your feet, pointed toward the target, and want you to square up to that. Then he would run a club perpendicular to it so you could get the ball positioned properly. He wanted your driver on your left heel and, say, a 7-iron in the middle of the stance. Of course, Mr. Penick was teaching a little bit of a hook, and when I went on the tour, I found I needed to hit the ball slightly higher than I could with the hook. Therefore, I moved the ball position slightly further forward. This allowed me to hit the ball on a higher trajectory. But one of the unexpected benefits was that the flight of the ball straightened out some.

Whenever he could, he would teach by example, a little show-and-tell, rather than words. One of the big problems many amateurs have is the so-called coming over the top. Mr. Penick would never use that phrase. He avoided language that might be misunderstood, that means one thing to you and something else to another player.

He would put a grass-cutter, a sickle, on the end of a golf shaft. It had a blade an inch wide, with sharp edges on both sides, that would lie flat against the grass. If you swung over the top, the sickle got stuck in the ground. This technique taught you to just clip the top of the grass. After you had swung a few times, Mr. Penick would put the golf club back in your hand and say, "Now swing the same way." It was so simple . . . and it worked.

Ben tells a similar story: "One day he was giving me a putting lesson, and he asked if I was pushing or pulling the ball. I said, 'I think I'm pulling.' After watching me hit a few putts, he went into the golf shop and brought out some talcum powder. He picked up the ball and sprinkled some powder on the back where the putter face would hit it. He then instructed me to hit some putts and inspect the face to see where the 'powder burns' were. Sure enough, it left a powder mark on the heel, not the center. I was pushing, not pulling!"

Ben later commented, "It was about as simple a trick as I've ever seen. His genius was in that clear-cut, non-mechanical way of teaching."

In my teens, the Austin Country Club had about the best collection of single-digit-handicap players anywhere in the state. And, of course, Texas had a tremendous reputation for producing better players than anywhere in the nation.

Why Texas? The conditions. We had so many different surfaces, hardened and coarsened by the winds and the rains and the harsh Texas sun; these were challenges that made you adapt. We are losing our edge now because our golf courses are in such splendid shape. If they were a little less well conditioned, the way they were in the old days, Texas players would still be dominating the sport. But everything is getting too cushy, and our courses now look like everybody else's. Of course, another reason why many Texans were such renowned golfers was that, in Austin, we had Mr. Penick, the best instructor around.

For the first few years after the Kites came to town in 1962, I wasn't close to being the best junior player at the club. There were fifteen- and sixteen-year-olds who could just thrash me, along with every other junior player in sight. Of course, they were older, and they were expected to beat me. But it gave you a lot of incentive.

I sought out Mr. Penick for instruction, or advice, whenever I came to the club, which was just about every day, certainly during the summer. He charged me for my first lesson, three dollars and fifty cents. From then on, he never charged me again. For a long time I tried to pay him, but finally I felt I might be offending him. That was just the kind of generous person he was. In his mind, a lesson was not thirty minutes on the practice tee. He felt that the lesson was ongoing, that it might last a lifetime. That was really the case. Some days he would stop by and watch me hit a couple of balls and walk away.

Wouldn't say a word about my game. That was a lesson, too. The message was: You are in a nice groove. Keep it up. Don't tinker. Other times he might spend a couple of hours with me each day.

He was never confrontational, though I'm sure I gave him an opportunity or two to lose his temper. One such instance comes to mind. I was out playing late one day with Dad, who had come to the club straight from work, and we only had time for nine holes. Getting such a late start, we were bringing in the flags. On our last hole, I missed a five-foot putt and, angrily, I reached out and hit the ball and took a divot in the green. It was the ninth green, and I still remember the pin placement, and that awful divot, as if it were yesterday.

Dad was so mad he told me I was going to have to tell Mr. Penick that I took a divot in *his* green. I begged him, "Dad, don't make me do that, don't make me tell Mr. Penick." I must have been about fourteen and I was scared to death, but Dad insisted: "We're not leaving until you tell him."

It was hard, really hard. But I went into the shop and Mr. Penick could see from looking at me that the punishment already had been inflicted. He said, "That's all right, Tommy. I'll go out and repair the green. Try not to do it anymore." He didn't have to tell me that: I wouldn't have dreamed of doing it again. Although he understood young tempers, you didn't want to test his compassion more than once, or twice.

Up to the time I turned seventeen, I really hadn't accomplished a heckuva lot. And then that year, 1966, I qualified for the National Junior Championship at Whittier, California. I was eliminated in the semifinals, along with Lanny Wadkins. That was the start of a nice friendship between us; our birthdays are four days apart, and from that time on, Lanny and I competed almost as much as Ben and I do. (In 1970, I would lose the U.S. Amateur title to Lanny by one stroke.)

My game stepped up, and I was becoming a real player. It wasn't as if I went from being a thirteen-year-old kid to seventeen overnight, but there was a nice progression. Playing well in California had given me some of the confidence I needed.

When I joined the golf team at the University of Texas, the coach was George Hannon, who had succeeded Mr. Penick. I am two years older than Ben Crenshaw, and in my junior and senior years we were ranked one or two on the team, based on how we had played the previous week. It was pretty cut-and-dried. That's one of the great things about golf. It is cut-and-dried. Whoever shot the lowest score in the last tournament was ranked Number 1. You keep the politics out of it, because 68 beats 69 or 75 beats 76 every time.

Occasionally, Mr. Penick would slip out and watch us play, but he would always kind of hang back and stay behind a tree. I only spotted him a couple of times at tournaments. I know he was at others, but mostly he kept

"Taking dead aim," as Harvey taught me, during the State Junior
Tournament in San Antonio, 1966 Courtesy of Tom Kite, Sr.

out of sight, always fretting that he would distract us. He was also trying to make a statement: "When they went out on the course, I had already taught them all I knew. After that they were on their own."

But in the clubhouse, or at the first tee, there was nearly always a telegram waiting, with three words: TAKE DEAD AIM!

Coach Hannon understood the special relationship Mr. Penick had with his students, and he handled it well. Hannon would bounce his ideas off Mr. Penick and see what he thought. After I went on tour, I came in contact with several great teachers, starting with Bob Toski, and later Peter Kostis, Chuck Cook, and Jim McLean, among others. It gave me an opportunity to fire questions at some of the best thinkers in the game, and I took advantage of it. But I knew in the back of my mind that "Harvey knows best." If Kostis, for example, said something that impressed me, the next time I got back to Austin I would run it by Mr. Penick.

He really enjoyed comparing theories. In terms of his own teaching, he liked my bringing other ideas to him. He was always a little concerned that I might get too analytical, too mechanical, rather than following my instincts, and at times I have. Intuitively, he knew this could be a pitfall for me. As he often said, you can think yourself into a slump; trust your instincts, be the kind of Texan who "doesn't need all day to look at a horseshoe."

As a kid, or at a lawn party, have you ever noticed how little time players take before they let the horseshoe fly? All they are doing is aiming at a post.

That was Mr. Penick's point. Other coaches enjoy the mind games, and they feel fulfilled when they find a player who sort of strip-searches his game before he can swing a club.

When I trust all my training, I play my best golf. So I had to go against my nature at times and not play the game in my head. For most of us, mechanical thoughts will ruin a good game.

Mr. Penick never saw me play in a PGA tournament except on television. The invitation was always there, but he never came. This didn't surprise me because I remember how he was during my amateur and college days. And besides, as the years passed, he didn't need anyone coming up to him to tell him what a great teacher or great person he was. He was living it. When his books came out, he enjoyed the accolades because they were affirmation for all the things he taught and believed in, but he did not need them to be happy.

Let me pause here for a moment. Now and again, I refer to Mr. Penick as Harvey to break up the repetition. But I could never call him that when he was alive, and it doesn't come naturally to me now that he isn't. Mainly, it was the way I was brought up—to show respect for my elders. And there was no one I respected more than Harvey Penick.

He always insisted, even into his nineties, that you called him Harvey. His usual retort was, "I'm not Mr. Penick. I'm his son Harvey."

I'm now at an age, forty-seven, where my kids' friends call me Mr. Kite. It reflects the way they were raised, but I don't think I will ever like it. I feel that way partly due to Mr. Penick's insistence on being addressed as Harvey. And I never could, which may not explain anything at all.

I think the way you feel comfortable addressing a person depends on the image the person projects. With some there is a distance, a dignity, a wall you can't get past. With others first names come naturally.

After I'd turned pro and went on the tour in 1973, I played a number of practice rounds with Sam Snead. When I called him Mr. Snead he walked over, draped an arm around my shoulder, and said, "Son, there ain't no Misters on the PGA Tour. Everybody here has a first name. Mine's Sam." So from then on I felt very comfortable calling him Sam. On the other hand, I never had the opportunity to compete against Byron Nelson and Ben Hogan, who were the same age as Sam. Therefore, when I see them they are Mr. Hogan or Mr. Nelson. But then again, Jimmy Demaret was from the same era, and he was always Jimmy. Even today there are members at the club—such as Ben's dad—whom I can never call anything but Mr. Crenshaw.

Even though I couldn't bring myself to use his first name, I never felt any uneasiness in the presence of Har-

I'd just turned pro, 1972. Courtesy of Tom Kite, Sr.

vey Penick. I was curious about him and what his life had been, but he talked very little about himself, nor did he include much personal history in his two most famous books. What I learned about him I learned from others, mainly his wife, Helen, and his son, Tinsley.

Harvey came along in an era of knickers and niblicks, a more romantic time of gaslights and cobbled streets, when a pro entered a clubhouse through the kitchen door, if he entered at all.

Mr. Penick was among the first of the homebred pros to take over from the Scotsmen and the Englishmen who were the game's first teachers in America. Herbert Warren Wind mentions him in his book *The Story of American Golf*. "If you want to look it up," Harvey would say if someone inquired, "it's in the revised edition." The remark struck a note both modest and scholarly.

By any reckoning, Harvey Penick was one of the great golf teachers of our time. Or his time. Which means, naturally, of any time. He was still giving lessons in his eighties, an age, as Casey Stengel once put it, "when you look around and a lot of your friends are no longer breathing."

Harvey's students and books have carried his name and message across the world. He is indelibly a part of the history of the sport, revised or otherwise. Here is a condensed history of this legendary coach:

At the age of eight, he began to caddie at the Austin

Country Club, as his older brothers had done before him. He wanted to begin sooner, but his mother refused to allow it until he started school. In those days, it was not unusual for a boy eight or older to be in the first grade.

He was promoted to the golf shop at twelve and became a club professional at eighteen. The year was 1923, and an English pro named Jim Smith left Austin for the opening of a new course in Denver, called Cherry Hills. Young Harvey had so impressed the club membership that the board of directors held the job open a month so he could graduate from high school. He never had time to be an amateur; he was already a pro with a job. He received a guarantee of fifty dollars a month, a percentage of what he sold in the shop, and whatever he earned from giving lessons.

When he entered college it was as a coach, not a student, at the University of Texas. He held the job for thirty-three years, taking no salary, while continuing to teach at the Austin Country Club, a position that lasted forty-eight years. He retired from the ACC in 1971, to be succeeded by Tinsley, and became the head professional emeritus. He still did odd jobs around the club—as well as teach a full schedule. But as he became more disabled, there was less he could do. Eventually he even worked as the starter. He knew that everyone who played that day had to visit with the starter, so he was able to keep up with his entire membership. But, of course, he always joked that it took him sixty years to "work my way down to the worst job at the club."

A golf course was to Mr. Penick what a park bench must have been to Bernard Baruch: an office, a front porch, a place to teach and take the sun and lay a little philosophy on those who happened his way. His wisdom and philosophy live on in his books, the first being the best-selling *Harvey Penick's Little Red Book*, which he published late in his life.

Given the glut of books containing golf tips, the runaway sales of Harvey's books caused something of a major upset in publishing. First, Harvey and his coauthor, Bud Shrake, made a smart marketing move. They insisted on having a small book, five inches by eight, because both knew that most golfers will pay twenty dollars for anything they can stick in the pocket of a golf bag.

The word of mouth from the pros and from the fans was huge. But my own opinion is that the red and green books caught fire because they had a Forrest Gumpian quality. When Harvey gave a tip on how to control your backswing, he said, "Imagine you are toting a bucket of water." Or take his observation about speed on the green: "I like to see a putt slip into the hole like a mouse." He spent sixty years collecting his thoughts and guidelines and insights, and these are among my favorites. He hated to see anyone act in a snobby way to those who were lower on the ladder. "We are frequently misjudged by our superiors," he said, "but never by our subordinates."

What he gave us was a way of thinking that went well beyond golf and reached people who are just crying for some simplicity. Most things are too complicated today.

It is ironic, I suppose, that he never had a high profile, was not known to the average golf fan, until the last years of his life. But those players whom the average fan idolized knew about him. Wherever they collected, he was quoted and talked about with a reverence rare in any sport.

"Even though I grew up in El Dorado, Arkansas, I went to the University of Texas in 1952 because of Harvey," said Davis Love, Jr. "If you went to an amateur tournament in the South and Southwest, you were certain to hear about him."

The elder Davis was a contender and actually was an early leader in the Masters in 1964, the same week his son and namesake was born. With his family expanding, he left the tour to become the assistant pro to Wes Ellis at Mountain Ridge Country Club, in New Jersey. There he was struck by a sudden, disturbing thought: He knew nothing about teaching someone to play golf. He did the obvious thing. He put in a call to Harvey Penick in Austin. As Love recalled the episode:

"I said, 'Mr. Penick, I'm up here now in New York and I've got about a month before the snow is off the ground and I have to start teaching folks. I've never taught before. What do I do?' He asked me, 'Have you ever played a musical instrument?' I said, no, I hadn't. He said, 'Go out and buy one, take two or three lessons, and call me back.'

"I went out and rented a clarinet. I couldn't afford to buy one. That was one reason I left the tour—I wasn't making enough money to buy luxuries. I found a woman who gave lessons out of her home. The day of my first lesson I drove up to her house, nervous and worried about doing the right thing, about embarrassing myself in front of her. I didn't know any musical terminology, and when the lesson began I wasn't sure what she was talking about. I went through all the things people feel when they're faced with any new learning experience— including a golf lesson.

"And then it hit me. This was what Harvey had in mind. He knew I had played golf since I was three and everything about the game came naturally to me. So I had to learn what it was like to be on the other side, to be a student."

The range of people who swung by Austin to see him was impressive. One day, after Harvey had semi-retired, a West Coast pro asked if he gave lessons to old people. The question startled him for just a moment.

"Well, sure," he said, and he proceeded to tell him about a club member named Jim Swearingen. "Eighty years old, same as me. I guess that's old, but I'm still giving him a lesson once a week." They had started when both men were thirty. "The only trouble," Harvey confided, "is if he pops the ball a little he can't see where it goes. He's like me. He can't see the ball unless he tops one about fifty yards."

When Harvey wasn't around, Mr. Swearingen worked with Tinsley Penick, who told the visiting pro from California, "Yeah, he has the same problem as my dad. They both still knock the ball out of sight."

Modesty and fairness were among the virtues Mr. Penick valued. Also, the satisfaction of teaching others to play was as real to him as the joy of playing. Although he would seldom admit it, his level of play was once quite high. In 1924, he began his professional career by beating Light Horse Harry Cooper in an exhibition match at the Austin Country Club. He held the course record there for years, with a 63, until it was broken by Jimmy Demaret. Harvey qualified for the U.S. Open and the PGA championship and once teamed with Ben Hogan on the Texas Cup team in the 1930s.

But he capsuled his playing career in one sentence: "The year I qualified for the National Open, I went up and saw Sam Snead drill one like a bullet, and on the train going home I decided I better specialize in teaching."

That typical touch of modesty ignored the fact that he probably had the ability to play close to Sam Snead's level. His decision to leave the tour, I believe, was based on his own awareness that he was born to teach. (Money never drove Harvey's wagon.) He also had a longtime love for Austin, a pretty, mellow college town he refused to leave for far more lucrative offers and prestige.

Obviously, he didn't have the strength that Sam had, but the stories about Harvey as a young man nearly always included a reference to his superb short game. If anyone ever heard him boast about anything, this was it.

He had a perfect putting stroke that he would go through in slow motion, almost like a playback on television. He was showing it to me on the putting green one day, when an amateur photographer happened to pass by and snap it. The picture hangs on my office wall.

Now, when Mr. Penick started listing the all-time great putters, he always talked about Kathy Whitworth and Ben Crenshaw and Horton Smith. But every once in a while he couldn't hold back, and you would hear him say, "I felt like I had the best ten-foot putting stroke in the game."

As we say in Texas, what Harvey did best was put the hay down where the mules can get at it. I can't be objective about this, but I like to think that he was pleased with the way Ben and I turned out. I know he enjoyed

You can tell it's the 1970s by the longish hair—mine, not Harvey's—and the checkered slacks. Eternal truth: It's called the short game. Work on it.

watching us. Everybody did. You had two kids growing up in the same town, who were ripping it up by the time they were seventeen or eighteen, beating most if not all of the local competition. Austin had a population of three hundred thousand and one country club of any significance. So, yeah, it was fun to be a part of what was happening.

Mr. Penick was careful to give us both all we needed. Never before had a golf instructor taken two kids from ground zero, basically, and helped them become as good as Ben and I became—without sacrificing one for the other. I find that incredible because I don't think there is another teacher who could have achieved the same results.

In almost every case, what you would have is a teacher with one student who fits his or her theories and one who does not. The latter becomes a sacrificial lamb. Harvey didn't play favorites. No teacher could rival the influence he had on such a variety of students. Ben and I are almost opposites in so many ways, our personalities, ideas, swings, with different strengths and weaknesses. The fact that we both became top-level players is a tribute to his coaching, that he didn't kill off the spirit in one of us to have the other succeed.

This brings to mind the sports psychologist from North Carolina, Dan Coop, who spent two days with Mr. Penick in Austin one year. He was curious about this very topic, Harvey's successes with Crenshaw and Kite. "How can you work with two such different types?" the man wanted to know.

"It's easy," said Harvey. "When I'm giving lessons to one, I don't let the other hang around."

WATER HOLE #1

In his original red, Scribbletex notebook, Harvey Penick jotted down his impressions of his students and his thoughts on teaching the game. Edited by another teaching pro, Betty Hicks, Harvey's "diary" appeared in several issues of *Golf Digest* in 1960. On this and other pages, his entries show how sharp his insights were sixty or more years ago:

Entry, February 20, 1925

No two golf pupils are alike. But there are pitfalls that seem to face three types of players. There do not seem to be too many exceptions:

1. Women listen too well and too often, especially to people who don't understand the golf swing. Everyone wants to give them advice.

2. The average man tries to play like a tournament player.

3. Tournament players—especially young ones—try to play like someone else instead of simply being themselves.

Happy after making a birdie on the seventh hole, I went on to win second place in the 1997 Masters at the Augusta National Golf Club. Tiger Woods, playing in his first Masters, led the field throughout, breaking all golf records. AP/Wide World Photos

Chapter Two

ONE COACH,
EIGHTEEN HOLES,
NO WAITING

Anyone who never met Harvey Penick might find it odd that so many memories of this pure and plain and patient soul have an offbeat quality. They are not always flattering, and the point is sometimes vague, but the stories reflect the tranquil way he moved through life.

His son Tinsley tells this one:

"There was a good-sized pit near the swimming pool of the Austin Country Club (at the Riverside Drive location), caused by erosion and the loss of a large tree or two. A member of the club, who had lost his larynx to cancer, was out walking his small Scotch terrier one morning, and the dog jumped in the pit. The man went in after him and couldn't climb out. Now they were both stuck.

"My dad, who had turned seventy, always went to work early, and he happened by, all bent over from his back problems, his hearing almost gone, deep in thought. He looked down, spotted them, and said, 'Joe, you better get out of there. You'll get poison ivy.' And he kept on walking to the pro shop."

It was a case of a man who couldn't hear being unable to rescue someone who couldn't speak. "It took two more hours for help to arrive, but it turned out fine, and Dad felt secure knowing his advice had been sound."

There have been so many apt descriptions of Harvey, repeated on so many occasions, that it is hard to know where to give the original credit. Herbert Warren Wind, I think, said his face had that "lived-in look." Harvey would have blushed if he knew someone had referred to him as "the Mother Theresa of golf"—not because of the gender, but because, seriously as he took his job, he never equated it with healing the sick or feeding the poor.

It was Dick Metz who said a club pro had to be half-mule and half-slave, but Harvey Penick defied the second part.

Golf is the most metaphysical of all sports, and Harvey understood this deep in his bones. A writer in Glasgow, Hugh MacDonald, described Harvey's teaching style as a combination of "Zen and the Art of Mashie Niblick Maintenance." He noted Harvey's fascination with Scot-

Harvey Penick, the subject of an NBC-TV special, at the Austin Country Club in February 1994 Gary Edwards

land and his saying, borrowed from Brigadoon: "On summer evenings when it stays light until an hour or two before midnight, whole families run out for putting in the town square."

There is poetry here, but also a quirk. Harvey had many invitations to visit Scotland and England and tread the great golf courses of those countries. He never went, although his wife, Helen, traveled to Europe four or five times with friends. Harvey couldn't see any reason to go, having traveled there so many times in his imagination. But he certainly was proud of the cashmere sweaters brought to him by many a club member. He especially liked the one with the St. Andrews logo on the chest.

He could be stubborn, but he grasped, as MacDonald put it, "the beautiful paradox of life: the only things you keep are those you give away." When Zen and yoga were in fashion in the 1960s, he applauded any golfer—later Greg Norman was one—who adopted these mental disciplines. Harvey had been using them, unaware that they had names, at least since the thirties, aware that to change your life, or your golf game, you have to change the way you think.

I have often wondered what it was about Harvey that inspired such a degree of respect and love. There are only limited ways to say that he was kind and wise and humble and forever giving. He was impossible to resist because he never gave off negative energy, sarcasm, or resentment. His silence was the silence of the forest, the lack of noise no indicator of all the activity within. He was in all ways a man of economy.

I suppose it was the mix of these qualities that touched so many people. But Harvey Penick wasn't meant to be explained or analyzed. He was meant to be enjoyed. So I will try to keep this light, if not breezy, and not put him under a microscope. That was the last place he would want to be, with the exception of being away from home.

If you look for deeper meanings in Harvey's work, you risk missing the gritty observations that frequently contained the lesson of the day. I don't mean he had a course plan. You just kept learning from him, as when he said, "If you can't break 80 you've no business on a golf course. If you can break 80 you probably have no business."

That line really registered with me. Over the years, I wondered how to tell my kids when I left the house each morning, with my clubs and my sunscreen, that daddy was going to his office.

Beginning in 1963, and through my graduation from Texas in 1972, I soaked up just about everything Harvey said. I actually looked forward to the bad weather days in Austin, when the cold and blustery rains cleared out the club. There might be two or three of us, or just me, hanging out with him in the shop. Those were the storytelling times, when he would talk about the game across the years, the great players and coaches. Harvey didn't object to a compliment now and then, but he always drew a line. If you mentioned an article in, say, *Golf Digest*, that called him the best golf teacher of all time, he would shake his head. That title, he'd say, belonged to Stewart Maiden, the pro at Atlanta's East Lake, whose heyday was in the 1930s. "He taught Bobby Jones and Glenna Collett Vare. A man may teach one kid who becomes great. But two like that is no accident."

Jones won golf's grand slam—the U.S. and British Opens, the U.S. and British Amateurs—in 1930, at the age of twenty-eight. He retired the same year. No one knew then that the handsome Georgian was suffering from a bone disease that would render him helpless and eventually kill him. Harvey considered Jones the greatest golfer who ever lived, and I don't think many historians disagreed with him.

Harvey talked little about his background, but you could pick up bits and pieces from Helen or Tinsley or his older friends.

The Penicks have their roots in England and Wales. Around 1860, they moved to America, settling in the Carolinas. Some followed the frontier to Texas. Harvey was born in 1904 in Austin, the youngest of five brothers, all of whom became caddies. Harvey was bright, but having gone to work at the age of eight, his ambitions as a student were limited.

Tinsley remembers remarking one day to Harvey that

his wife had gone through high school with all A's and one D. Harvey laughed and said that meant he had one thing in common with his daughter-in-law: "I, too, only made one D in high school; all the rest were Cs."

But brains were not lacking in the family. Dr. Dan Penick, Harvey's double first cousin, taught Greek at the University of Texas. Harvey was self-educated as to college; he could not have found a better teacher. He turned down an appointment to West Point. He knew what his life's work was going to be.

He idolized his oldest brother, Tom, who had been a marine in World War I and worked briefly as a surveyor in the Pacific Northwest. When Tom was the head caddy at the Austin Country Club, he took care of his younger brothers. It was not uncommon for caddies to fight for jobs and for the older ones to beat up the smaller ones. But Tom was scary-tough, and no one messed with the Penick boys.

Between them, Harvey and Tom practically founded public golf in Austin. Tom left the caddy shack at Austin Country Club to become the head pro at the Lions Municipal course in 1929, a job he held until his retirement in 1961. In 1929, the Lions Muny was little more than a rocky pasture. But that year Tom Penick upgraded the course by enlisting the aid of the Civilian Conservation Corps, whose director was the father of Betsy Rawls. They got rid of the rocks, brought in river bottom soil,

There is definitely a family resemblance: My mom, Mauryene, and I toast
Mr. Penick at a 1992 dinner in his honor at the Austin Country Club.

and covered the course with a fine layer of fertile loam,
transforming it into pretty much the course it is today.

As the country was sliding into the Depression, Tom
and Harvey were building a modest golfing empire. They
developed and operated their own nine-hole course, with
sand greens. Most courses in the state back then had no
grass around the greens. When Tom decided to put in
Bermuda-grass greens in 1924, Harvey convinced the
board at Austin Country Club to do the same.

Their father—called Pap, a laborer much of his life—

helped out sometimes at their municipal course in the "pro shop," a small shed not much bigger than an out-house.

In addition, they owned a driving range with flood-lights on land overlooking Lake Austin. The brothers took turns running the place. Tom had a good head for business and sold the nine-hole course and the driving range several times because buyers would acquire one or both properties, then default on the payments, and Tom would repossess them. (Finally the course was sold and a municipal auditorium later occupied the site.)

But Harvey kept a hard schedule, working days at the Austin Country Club and nights at the range. What made the workload even more difficult was the fact that he was now a married man.

Harvey first scouted Helen Holmes in 1924, in the choir of the Hyde Park Christian Church, from his seat next to his mother in the back row. Helen was eighteen, one of six daughters of a minister. All of the girls went to college, in an era when many women did not.

In the Amazing Coincidence category, Helen's grand-father, known as Preacher Horn, performed the cere-mony when my mom's parents were married in the tiny town of McKinney, Texas. Golf was not part of their religion. Helen's dad, the Reverend Holmes, gave up af-ter one lesson from his son-in-law.

Helen giggles even now, some seventy years later and

two years after his death, when she tells how she and Harvey met:

"I learned that he came to church again the next week, but I don't remember noticing him. At that time I was taking classes at the University of Texas, and he rolled up beside me one day on my way to school, driving a long Nash roadster, a car he bought from his brother Tom. He had on knickers and a sport coat. He was real timid and almost in a whisper, he said, 'Can I take you to the campus?' I didn't know him and I said, 'No, thank you, I'm almost there.'

"I asked around about who he was. A few days later he saw me downtown and parked his car and came over to me. He asked if he could call me on the phone and I said, 'Yes, you may.' I'm embarrassed to say this, but he said he thought I was beautiful. He really did fall for me. I came home and fifteen minutes later he called.

"We had gone out to a couple of movies, when he asked me if I would go with him to San Antonio to see the Texas Open at Brackenridge Park. I never had so much as seen a golf course. I was just thrilled at the idea of going to San Antonio. When he picked me up I had on high heels, and he told me I better change to walking shoes, and I did.

"When we got there, we were walking onto the first tee, and who should be coming toward us but Bob Hope and Bing Crosby. Here I was at a golf tournament for

The Penicks celebrate a truly golden wedding anniversary.
Courtesy of Tinsley Penick

Helen and Harvey Penick: Still holding hands after all those years
Courtesy of Tinsley Penick

the first time in my life, and the first thing I saw was two famous movie stars, with a couple of policemen on either side to get them through the crowd. They were playing in the Pro-Am, although I didn't know what that was then. I squealed and cried out and Harvey had to tell me you were supposed to speak softly around the golfers.

"They didn't have a golf course in Cisco, the little town in West Texas where I came from. It wasn't a very popular sport back then, which was 1924. But Harvey started taking me out to the club, and I watched some of the members practice. We decided we were going to get married and we did, within a year. I just thought, well, I'll take it up after we get married.

"When we married, people kind of looked down on golf pros. In that era, when they played at a tournament they came in through the back door of the clubhouse or the kitchen. When Harvey asked me to marry him, he was worried that my father wouldn't give his permission. He said, 'Mr. Holmes may not want his daughter to marry a poor ol' golf pro.' But nobody in Austin ever looked down on Harvey Penick. They treated him like a king, always. And my dad never worried about Harvey making a living.

"He loved people and they loved him. He didn't see a lick of difference between the governor and a shoeshine boy. We were married during the Depression and I thought Harvey was rich. He was drawing a good salary from the club and some months he made four hundred dollars. He worked like a tiger. Cleaned the clubs, picked up the balls, cut the greens, gave the lessons, kept the inventory in the pro shop. I rarely worked in the shop and I would advise any young pro's wife against it. Sometimes when Harvey had to be somewhere else and no one else was around, I helped out. When customers came in I always had to warn them, 'If you buy anything you'll have to open the cash register because I don't know how.' Everyone who came to the shop treated me wonderfully.

"I was never very good at golf, even though I played all the time and had a lot of fun. When I played in ladies' tournaments I used my maiden name because when I went as Helen Penick people expected me to be so much better than I was. Harvey used to give me an occasional lesson. He'd spend ten minutes with me and say, 'You're doing pretty good, keep that up. Mr. So-and-So over here has a problem and needs my help.' And that was the end of my lesson."

Harvey's initial judgment of Helen was right, as it so often was in many things. Helen must have been beautiful then because she still is today, with soft blue eyes and a lilting southern accent. She still walks up to two miles a day, still drives, and has the robust health that was sadly denied her husband for so many years. She has traveled with friends to the Fiji Islands and taken two bus trips across the country. She still laments the fact that Harvey so rarely left Austin.

He did leave a few times, mostly in the 1960s, spending two summers at Cherry Hills in Denver and one in Monterrey, Mexico, partly to take a break from the relentless Texas heat. But he was always eager to get back to his club members and his University of Texas players.

He said he coached the team without taking a salary in order to get tickets to the University's football games and the swimming meets. The truth was he really couldn't resist the chance to do more teaching, and in the early years, there wasn't money in the school's budget for the golf team. When they traveled, the players often bunked four or more to a room in cheap motels.

If ever a man was a creature of habit and routine, it was Harvey Penick. He played golf just about every day. For a change of pace, he would go on fishing trips, usually with Wilmer Allison, the Texas tennis coach, and while they waited for a fish to bite the two of them would talk about the rules of golf.

He did not make sudden changes in his lifestyle, but he did make adjustments where necessary. He never smoked and, except for a polite glass of beer, didn't touch alcohol. Then, at the age of eighty-five, he developed a taste for wine. My guess is it had less to do with sophistication than with the pain that was his constant companion.

When Tinsley and Kathryn, Harvey's daughter, were

A 1940s Penick family portrait: big sister, Kathryn (left), *Harvey, and Helen holding an 18-month-old Tinsley* Courtesy of Tinsley Penick

growing up, the big family outing each year was to Dallas for the Texas-Oklahoma football game in early October. The rivalry between the two state schools, on either side of the Red River, was the oil and cactus country's version of Harvard and Yale. The Penicks would get up before dawn, drive to Dallas, check out the state fair, watch the football game, take in a play at night (the kind that would star Mary Martin), then drive home. Harvey never wanted to stay overnight. They did this every October from the late 1940s through the 1950s, until the kids went off to college.

When Tinsley was thirteen, they lived in a house on

the golf course at the Austin Country Club, which was then almost out in the country. At one time there was a barn behind the pro shop and a cow pen at the back of the house, to the left of the Number 12 tee. Harvey's brother Tom owned the land next to the shed, so Tinsley grazed a few cows there. Kathryn kept a horse, but the pastoral life was disrupted one day when the horse broke away and ran all over the greens. That caused quite a stir around the club.

When his children were growing up, Harvey had been good enough to play on the Texas Cup teams, and he had a nice run as a trick-shot artist, a talent he—and others of his day, like Ben Hogan—developed as a kid. Clubs around the country would invite him to put on a show. Harvey did a whole comedy act, using such props as rubber-shafted clubs hanging out of his bag, and he would add a flourish to his usual dapper attire. (Even when he was dressed normally, in a coat and tie and knickers and twill cap, all in loud golfer colors, Kathryn would hide in the back seat when he drove her to school.)

Another of his tricks involved a right-handed golf club with the back chiseled off so he could spin it around and swing left-handed. He would also hit the ball with his eyes closed. Such tricks were sometimes helpful in giving a lesson. For example, people tend to keep their heads down too much, so he would say, "You don't need to

Tinsley Penick didn't mind letting his dad drive the cart, even when Harvey was in his late eighties. Courtesy of Tinsley Penick

stare at the ball. Let me show you something." Then he would spin around and hit it with his eyes closed. This technique actually enabled him to teach the game to the blind.

He played quality golf until about 1960. To this day, Ben Crenshaw remembers seeing Harvey hit a drive that was the longest shot he had ever seen. Ben was only eight, but he says he was just awestruck. Then Harvey's many teaching obligations caught up with him. He found time for a round now and then, but more and more he used his clubs only to give lessons.

Despite his dedication to the game of golf, Harvey

was always a patriot and regretted the fact that he was too young when America entered the first World War and two years too old for the second. Even so, he tried to enlist after Japan bombed Pearl Harbor. The army rejected him because of his hay fever and sinus problems, which were so severe that doctors had to open his nasal passages with surgical instruments. These, you reflect, are not conditions ideal for a man who spent his life around grass and trees.

When you think about Harvey's longevity, the numbers are astounding. When Francis Ouimet won the U.S. Open in 1913, Harvey had already caddied for a year at the Austin Country Club. From the time he was eighteen, he went to the golf course every day it was open, seven days a week, working from dawn to dark. Add up the years from 1923 to 1990, and it is clear that nobody could have put more hours into a job. And on an hourly basis, could it possibly have been profitable?

Always a self-effacing man, turned off by immodesty, toward the end of his life Harvey experienced unaccustomed emotions after the runaway success of his *Little Red Book*. (Three others, *And If You Play Golf, You're My Friend*, referred to as his *Little Green Book*; *The Game for a Lifetime*; and *For All Who Loved the Game*, all written with Bud Shrake, soon followed.) He was briefly in a state of near giddiness. "One night," said Helen, "I heard him in the living room telling someone how many copies his book had sold. I yelled out to him, 'Harvey, you can't do that! That's boasting!' "

But no one begrudged him these moments of elation, considering that for the last two dozen years of his life, the one constant in his life was pain. He really did run a mom-and-pop operation, and at the end of the day here was the world's greatest golf teacher picking up balls on the driving range. His most serious health problems began one day in 1974 when some kids were beating him to the balls at the edges, tossing them into sacks, and running off. He could not abide stealing, and he jumped into a cart and took off after them. The cart struck a bump and he was thrown out, breaking his back. Tinsley found him lying on a concrete slab behind the pro shop. The temperature had risen to over 100 degrees that day.

From the time Harvey got out of the hospital, he never again had a full night's sleep. Usually he slept for an hour at a time. Whenever he moved, the pain in his back would wake him. He had operations to repair his back. Others followed to remove his appendix and his prostate and to treat a hernia and ulcers. He suffered terrible stomachaches, when the only way he could get any relief was to curl up on the floor, before he discovered that ulcers were the cause.

He went to work every day against this background of pain but made up his mind to live with it. The back problem was a degenerating one, but he kept his complaints to himself.

And then after his prostate surgery (a very unusual operation for someone of Harvey's advanced years), his health deteriorated to the point that doctors considered nursing care essential. He had spent five weeks in a hospital where his condition was often touch and go and he weighed only 110 pounds. When he pulled through he was depressed and confined to a wheelchair, but even so he refused to spend his money on a private nurse; he was keeping it for Helen and his family.

This was in 1990, before his first book was published, and a few club members and some of Harvey's students, including Ben and me, held a fund-raiser to enable Harvey to have nursing care around the clock. We considered our gift the least we could do, and as a result of the constant care, gradually his strength and his spirits returned. He underwent physical therapy, which involved bobbing up and down in a heated pool with a lot of elderly ladies. He hated every minute, but he did it.

His final days, and Ben's dramatic victory at the Masters, are part of his legacy, and I'll tell you about those later. But the examples he set for us were not just of his courage but of his compassion. He always took an interest in us and despite his physical pain insisted on being driven to the course in his golf cart whenever possible, taking his pain along for the ride. For so long it had been Mr. Penick who spared and comforted others. Now it was our turn to do what we could for him.

He put it on the record in his books that "Ben and

Ben Crenshaw's dramatic victory at the 1995 Masters is part of Harvey's legacy. José María Olazabal of Spain, the 1994 winner, helps him on with his green jacket. A two-time Masters champion, Ben's first win was in 1984. Reuters/Gary Hershorn/Archive Photos

Tommy were like sons to me." The fact is, there was another young Austin golfer who had an earlier place in his heart, Morris Williams, Jr.

Morris, Sr., was a typesetter at the *Austin American-Statesman,* and he wrote the newspaper's golf column too. But no one doubted that Morris, Jr., earned his own headlines. He was a special player and a charismatic person. He graduated from the University of Texas in 1953 and had been in the ROTC (Reserve Officers Training

Corps) to prepare for the Air Force, which offered a short-term enlistment or the long-term career of a pilot. He chose the latter, thinking he could save enough money to sponsor himself on the PGA Tour. There wasn't big money to be made on the tour in the 1950s, and the Hogans, Sneads, and Demarets commanded most of it.

Morris played golf in the service with both Dow Finsterwald and Arnold Palmer. Finsterwald told Harvey, and others, that Morris could have been every bit as good as Arnold.

But Morris, Jr., never had the chance to prove it. He was on a training exercise, diving at a target, and wasn't able to pull up fast enough. In the hope that Harvey could cushion the blow to the family, an Air Force officer placed the first call to the pro shop at the Austin Country Club. Harvey had to tell Morris Williams, Sr., about the crash.

In his office, Morris, Sr., looked up from the newspaper he was reading and he began to turn pale. He knew that Harvey Penick *never* left the golf course during the day, so the news had to be bad. "What has happened to Morris, Jr.?" he asked.

When he was told, he fainted right into Harvey's arms.

Helen had to carry the news to Mrs. Williams, who broke down, went wild, and actually took a swing at Helen. Neither parent ever got over the death of their son.

As the years passed, when Harvey singled out Ben and me, I always knew that a third name was special to him. He wasn't asking us to carry anyone else's bag. He wanted us to understand that life was fragile and a long career was a gift. And that we had to be Ben or Tommy and no one else.

WATER HOLE #2

February 28, 1930

There are not too many things that all fine golfers do in common. But players I'd like to play like observe three fundamentals:

1. They have good position to the ball.
2. They all pause momentarily at the top. I'd rather call it "gathering the swing together" than pausing.
3. They all have a little waggle or a forward press.

I get a kick out of discussing golf with J. K. Wadley, an oilman from Texarkana. He knows as much about the golf swing as anyone I've met, pro or amateur. He mentioned a boy from Fort Worth he'd like to see go somewhere in golf. If J. K. says the boy has the ability, I don't even have to see him swing to believe it.

I hope I recall his name right as being Nelson—Byron, I think.

Ben Crenshaw and me on the eighteenth green after the NCAA Golf Championship in Cape Coral, Florida, in 1972. We tied for first place, and rules didn't allow for a play-off. AP/Wide World Photos

Chapter Three

THE BEST OF
RIVALS

All through my amateur years, and for at least the first
third of my pro career, I was defined by what, and who,
I was not. I was not tall, not colorful, not long off the
tee, and not Ben Crenshaw.

I never found any of this strange. I didn't especially
enjoy it, but I understood. The pressure on the writers,
and the fans, to compare the two of us was not only
tempting; it was darned near mandatory.

The story was such a rich one: two young guys who
came along at the same time, almost out of the same
mold, who spent three decades on the same track, in the
same circle, under the same coach. Through it all, we
have stayed friends, a fact that a few observers may have

missed. Our friendship has gone on far longer than most vendettas and even most friendships.

We have had a wonderful rivalry, if you consider what we have a rivalry. In Texas, when you really trust someone, the saying is "He'll do to ride the river with." Ben and I have ridden the river for most of our lives, sometimes against the current, more often with the wind to our backs. There has never been anything mean-spirited between us. It has been a fun ride, a great and charming thing to have.

But despite our obvious friendship, the temptation is always out there to hope for a blood feud—the stuff of novels where there is nearly always a good guy and a villain. I don't mean this harshly, but media people tend to want everybody to choose sides. It makes good copy.

Now, when I was thirteen, and I won't kid about this, I was disheartened at times by these comparisons with Ben. It was tough. You want to take it out on somebody and you look around and you see a kid you can't get mad at and he's eleven years old. I remember an article that appeared in *Sports Illustrated* when we were in college, the whole gist of which was that Ben had the girls and the glamour and I was the guy who wore glasses and had pink skin and kinky hair. By the time you're thirty, you take it in stride and realize that it's all part of the circus.

At this point in our careers, the media has finally snapped to the fact that Ben is not going to say a whole

We three: Ben and I flank Harvey Penick after he received the Jimmy Demaret Award in 1989.

heckuva lot against me, and I'm not going to say a whole heckuva lot against Ben. Harvey set an example for us by ignoring the reporters' comments. He expected us to use our own good judgment.

This is not forced and it's not phony. We really like each other and each other's company. We were never Hope and Crosby, Butch and Sundance, Truman and Dewey. We were certainly not Palmer and Nicklaus because we haven't dominated our time in the same way. It's unlikely that two golfers will capture the masses as

Arnie did or the world of commerce as Jack did—unless Tiger Woods does both.

But I do believe we had a niche of our own. People who were close to golf enjoyed following us, I think, because of the contrast in our styles and temperaments. It was always Crenshaw and Kite, Natural Ability versus Hard Work. No one would deny that Ben is more of a showman. I'm like a guy laying bricks. When my buddy Bruce Lietzke was asked to name Tom Kite's closest friend on the tour, he answered, "His practice bag."

What has sustained the interest in the two of us for all these years is the fact that we both have enjoyed terrific careers. And we really don't appear to have changed much physically since we both left the University of Texas campus. (Maybe it was because we always looked so young next to Harvey Penick.) That isn't meant as conceit. It's true of most golfers. In no other sport do you see guys stay so much in the same physical form from Day One to the day they hang it up.

A golfer's temperament may change, may become calmer. But you don't see a pro golfer at 150 pounds one year and 200 the next. There is a reason, of course, why golfers maintain their weight. A large weight gain could have a significant impact on your game because it is not a sport of brute force. In most other sports, you put on, say, fifteen pounds, it makes you obviously bigger, stronger, maybe even faster. In golf, you put on fifteen pounds and you may lose your touch around the greens. Your timing is different. Your swing changes.

You see it when kids go through adolescence. They have grown a foot overnight, or so it seems, and they are hitting the ball twenty or thirty yards farther than last year. But they don't know where their swing is or where the ball is going.

In terms of personality, I don't think Crenshaw and Kite have changed much in the ways that are really noticeable. We still have a great loyalty to each other and the people around us, and we owe that to Mr. Penick's influence. When Ben's first marriage was breaking up, he stopped by my house one night to visit. We went down to the workshop in my basement. He didn't exactly spill his guts, but we worked on our clubs and talked. If you knew Ben, you could tell it was a hurting time. (Ben remarried, and he and Julie have two little girls who are knockouts. Ben is as contented now as I have ever seen him.)

In terms of competition, it is a curious truth that on the tour you are battling every day against people who are your close friends. The same goes for attorneys, who go out and have dinner together, but in the courtroom the venom drips from their lips and they go for the jugular. If the other guy doesn't understand this, he doesn't understand his job.

So even though there is a fine camaraderie among the pros and hanging around the locker room is pure fun, you have to seal yourself away from the others at some point. You need to do a lot of meditating and focus on yourself, because as friendly as Ben and I are, he pulls for the kid named Crenshaw and I pull for the one named Kite.

Always popular among his colleagues, even today Ben is considered the most likable guy on the tour. He is one of those rare people who are able to make everyone they come in contact with feel good. Arnold Palmer can. Harvey Penick could. And Ben Crenshaw belongs on that list. He has the gift.

I never resented all the attention paid to Ben. But as Darrell Royal, the longtime Texas football coach, used to say, "You may not believe in beauty contests, but if you're in one, you want the judges to vote you purty."

Christy and I were married in 1975, in her parents' backyard in Las Vegas, where she had taught school. When we came home to Austin to start our life together, the environment puzzled her. Keep in mind, Christy had lived in Las Vegas, so she knew how winning and losing can turn otherwise normal souls a little crazy. "I was amazed," she said, "that people felt they had to choose sides. Even at the club, where they grew up, the members were divided. You were Tom's friend or you were Ben's. It was as though they were running on different tickets. People felt they couldn't root for both of them."

Ben and I are the proud bookends in this photograph—taken in the mid-1980s—with the people's choice, Lee Trevino (second from left), and the legendary Ben Hogan.

Today I wouldn't trade anything for the competition I had with Ben. It helped both our games. When I started on the tour, I know there were those who doubted I would make it . . . whatever making it means. A lot of that was based on the fact that Ben was considered a better player than I was in college. But, really, not by much. In my senior year, we competed in thirteen tournaments. He won seven, I won five, and we tied for the NCAA individual title.

There was a time in the 1980s when Ben was confused

about his game and was in a fearsome slump. He took some hits. Some people said he was too preoccupied with golf's past to take care of the here and now. But everyone tried to help him, and anyone but Ben might have been suspicious of their motives.

It was always hard for Ben to say, "No, thanks, I don't need your help." Some members of the press picked up on this and viewed his good nature as a weakness. This made Ben wonder, *Is it a compliment if niceness is said to be your weakness?* One day I told him to find one person he had confidence in and not to listen to anyone else. Even as I said that, I realized I was giving him more advice.

Ben had an impressive winning record and knew he could win again. In fact, he won the first tournament he played for money, at twenty-two—the 1973 Texas Open. "I never felt any pressure to live up to what the press wrote or the public thought," he said. "All my pressure was always from within. I was an early bloomer and at some point progress comes hard."

The one man he needed to help him out of his slump, as he later readily admitted, was Harvey Penick. He wasn't getting home that often, between playing the tour and making appearances. The weeks turned into six months. Then he made it back to Austin and the practice tee. Recalled Ben, "Harvey said, 'Before we do anything else, let me see your swing.' I hit four or five balls and he stopped me. He put his hand on my shoulder and said, in about as harsh a tone as he ever used, 'Ben, don't *ever* wait this long again to come back and see me.' "

That was the only day they spent on the course during Ben's visit. One rainy afternoon they sat in the pro shop for three hours just visiting, talking. They talked about Ben's days at Texas, his family, his library of golf books. Harvey told him to put the disappointments of that year (1985) behind him. He told him to go back to the swing God gave him. "Hogan and Harry Vardon had long swings, like Ben," said Harvey. "Bobby Jones was every bit as long. I told Ben to ignore any criticism of his swing; that God gave him two ears, let all that advice go in one and out the other."

Of course, Ben had a lot more winning ahead of him. Currently, we have the same number of titles, nineteen, which makes a compliment Ben paid me a few years ago all the nicer. He said that in our careers, I had passed him. I don't really know if that is true. I think mine may have been more consistent. But Ben has known those Mount Everest highs: witness his two wins in the Masters in 1984 and 1995—the latter one for Harvey, whose memory spurred him on that day.

Ben's victory that week in April in Augusta was one of the great acts of rising to the occasion in the history of any sport, and, of course, I'm not the only one to think so. We had flown back to Augusta for the Masters together on a chartered plane after being pallbearers at Harvey's funeral on Wednesday, not knowing how either of us would react.

We had both lost a lifelong friend and teacher, a second father figure. I missed the cut. Ben went on to play inspired golf, in the most emotional week of his career, to win his second Masters. It was a real tribute to Ben that he played with such drive and desire. I believe this was a case where, once his game began to click, he used the emotion to his advantage. He handled it far better than I did. My hat is off to him.

There are two kinds of momentum. At the 1995 Masters, Ben felt the one that lifts you along on silken wings. He said he felt Harvey guiding him, and you could not disprove it by the way he played. Then there is a negative kind of momentum that sucks you in like quicksand. If you are not playing well, and I wasn't, if you are not feeling inspired, it can be a difficult time. A crisis or heartache isn't really what you need.

Ben's first win at Augusta, in 1984, was one I watched up close and personal. I led the tournament in the last round by three strokes, only to have it snatched away by Ben, playing just ahead of me. People think I blew it when I went in the water on Number 12. That isn't so. I lost because I missed some crucial putts early in the round. Still, I played well enough to have been able to win. I had no control over the fact that Ben made a sixty-five-foot putt on the tenth hole. He was in three-putt range and he made the putt. That's Ben.

Losing anytime, but especially after you have led for three rounds, is a test of character. Harvey helped me get through it; he never let you hang your head. Of course, he was ecstatic for Ben, and I'm sure he told him what he deserved to hear. That was the easy part.

The difficult part is to reassure the guy who didn't win. Harvey stressed the good things about my game: Look how well you played all week. Except for one or two holes, you could have won very easily. Let's not dwell on those one or two holes where you slipped up. As he always had, he impressed on me that you need to have a very short-term memory of the bad moments and a long-term memory of the good.

I was grateful for what Ben's dad said a few days later. "If there is anyone who deserves to win," said Charlie Crenshaw, "if hard work is really supposed to pay off, then it's Tom."

The Crenshaws and the Kites used to play Sunday foursomes in Austin when Ben and I were in junior high, the fathers against the sons. As time went on, they gave us fewer and fewer strokes. The dads won about half the time, then a little less. Then the games tapered off as the kids moved on.

No matter what has been said or written, I don't care to characterize our status among Harvey's students. I'm

*A father-and-son team at the 1981 Bing Crosby National Pro-Am
at Cypress Point: Dad and I placed second that year.*
Courtesy of Tom Kite, Sr.

not being coy. He didn't do rankings. His most important student was the one standing in front of him at that
moment. But I do believe we were the ultimate tribute
to his skills as a teacher.

No golf teacher has ever achieved the level of success
that Harvey achieved with two people as opposite as Ben
and me. There are instructors who work with numerous
top professionals and amateurs. For example, David Led-
better teaches Nick Price, Nick Faldo, and Greg Norman.
But they were accomplished players when they came to
work with him. David did not teach them from the time
they were pups, as Harvey did us.

Harvey, with characteristic modesty, never claimed
credit for anyone's success, including the great golfers
whose careers he made or saved. There was nothing
about the man to dislike, but he may have attracted a
touch of jealousy from some of the teaching pros.

Once, after speaking at a PGA seminar in Georgia,
Harvey was stopped by a club pro looking for an argument. "Those guys who played for you at Texas," the pro
said, "they were good players before they ever got to
college, isn't that right?"

"Yes, sir, that's true," said Mr. Penick.

"This Crenshaw kid, he had a name for himself before
he ever went to college, right?"

"Yes, sir."

Now a crowd started to form.

"You didn't have a lot of teaching to do with Crenshaw. He was already a complete player in college, right?"

"Yes, sir," said Harvey, starting to walk away.

"Tell me," said the pro, pressing his luck, "when was the first time you worked with Crenshaw?"

"I believe he was five years old when his father brought him around," replied Harvey without a touch of anger.

If the pro had quit one question earlier, Mr. Penick would have been perfectly willing to let him think that he had upstaged a legend. Harvey had an ego the size of a pinpoint.

These and other thoughts were out there in the ozone, I suppose, when Ben and I joined each other at Champions Golf Club in Houston, in September of 1996, to tape a match for Shell's *Wonderful World of Golf* series.

It was meaningful for both of us because our generation grew up watching the original shows. There were ninety-two matches filmed between 1961 and 1969, before Shell reduced its sponsorship, and I think Ben has copies of most of them. Dave Marr, another Texan, was the commentator, along with Jack Whitaker of ABC.

The producer was Terry Jastrow, one of Harvey's pupils and among my best friends when we were both growing up. He worked at the Austin Country Club and went on to win a Texas junior title and a scholarship to the University of Houston. He didn't make it to the tour, but he covered it for years on television as the senior producer for golf at ABC Sports.

This is what Terry remembered about our summer afternoons at the ACC: "Harvey would send us out to the far end of the practice tee to hit balls. Most people would hit balls from regulation-size wire buckets. Tom and I used to hit tractor baskets full of golf balls. Then Tom would go out and hit some more."

Unbelievably, that summer at Champions was the first time in our pro careers, in twenty-plus years, that Ben and I had gone head-to-head, one-on-one. There was pride at stake, but the tension you feel in a tournament was absent. We both had our share of victories and defeats, had both played well at the same courses but in different years. As juniors, and collegians, we had squared off regularly.

We would have preferred that we had been playing closer to our prime. Most of the original shows were between rivals who were at the top of their form. So this was not the first time or the last time or the ideal time for us to play together, but we did feel all the sentiment that the romantics among us wanted.

It was very relaxed, a treat to play someone with whom I'd formed a close bond through the years. I knew that the two of us felt a huge amount of respect and affection for each other.

We played a practice round the day before the match with Jackie Burke, Jr., the son of the legendary golf teacher and the 1956 Masters champion. Jackie had built Champions with Jimmy Demaret and a business partner, Pat Morgan.

Jackie's dad had been the pro at the prestigious River Oaks Country Club in Houston in the years before World War II. Burke, Sr., had learned the game in the east, from the Scotsmen who were the first major influence on golf in this country. Jackie remembers doing his homework while Harvey Penick sat in the living room of their home, listening to Jack, Sr.

"Harvey could go out every day and shoot 75, 75, 75," said Jackie. "Whack. Whack. Whack. He didn't take many chances. Dad told him, 'Harvey, if you want to shoot something besides 75, you need to deconstruct a little.' "

As we played our practice round, we had a fresh chance to admire what Burke has done at Champions. The course is basically a showcase for what golf is all about. Jackie keeps improving it, which means he didn't just build a course thirty years ago so he could sit on it. Champions will be a great test for years to come.

Ben wasn't hitting the ball especially well, and Jackie and I were both trying to help him with his swing. I wasn't putting well, and both of them tried to help me. And so it went.

Burke told us stories that day about *Wonderful World*, including his own first appearance in 1959 in some bitter cold weather in western Canada. It took three days to film the match.

He talked about his old mentor and partner, Jimmy Demaret, one of the regular voices on the telecast in the

1960s, along with Gene Sarazen. The series took Jimmy around the world. "It's really a travelogue," Jimmy once said, "but with class. You never get the feeling that you're selling gas."

One of the trips took Demaret to Guatemala, where Gardner Dickinson and Mason Rudolph were to match strokes. Arriving at his hotel, Demaret checked into his room, looked out the window, and witnessed a rare tourist attraction: an erupting volcano. Specifically, it had erupted over the golf course, and he thought that Shell might have the distinction of being the first to cancel a golf match on account of lava. The next day the course was covered with dust. The day after that, the winds blew much of it away, and they played on whatever was left.

The day following our practice round, Ben and I stepped onto the first tee at Champions, in front of the cameras and a gallery that included five thousand Shell employees and a crowd of our own friends.

I enjoyed the fact that the course wasn't roped off, so the gallery could walk with us in the old tradition of golf. There was chitchat with kids and friends and people I hadn't seen in a long time.

Addressing the crowd, Ben said, "I can't believe we're a part of this. So many people our age grew up watching these matches. I really wanted to be a part of it . . . especially here."

When I spoke to the crowd, I said, "This is a tremendous thrill for both of us to come back to Champions. To get a chance to play against Ben is always exciting. Plus, I'd like to beat him once or twice in my life."

I didn't beat him that day. In fact, neither one of us played very well, which was disappointing. Ben did have his touch around the greens, while I struggled with my putter. On the first hole, Crenshaw chipped in from the fringe twenty-five feet away for a birdie, setting the tone for the front nine. He then added another thirty-foot chip-in for a second birdie on Number 2, and I yanked my second putt left of the cup for a bogey. I winked at a small boy in the crowd and asked, "Why didn't you tell me it broke that way?" But I knew I pulled it.

For all intents and purposes, the match was over, and I spent the rest of the round trying to make the score respectable. That I was able to do. On Number 9, my second shot landed on the front of the green, and I drained a seventy-footer for an eagle three, the highlight of my round. Ben ended up shooting 69 to my 73.

I'm not a good judge of what kind of show we put on, but I felt a twinge of pride in simply being there. Here was Ben, now forty-four, still with the shaggy blond hair and engaging smile, sweet-tempered, wholesome as baked bread. And here was Tommy Kite, forty-six, determined to prove he could win again on the PGA Tour.

At one time it had been considered rare for a golfer to excel past the age of forty. Nicklaus won three PGA

*Just to prove you can win after forty! Jay Haas and me after winning
the Shark Shootout tournament in Thousand Oaks, California, 1996.*
AP/Wide World Photos

events after his forty-first birthday, Palmer once after he turned forty-two. However, in recent years superb golfers like Greg Norman, Hale Irwin, and Raymond Floyd are regulars on the tour. Raymond and Hale are marvels, still playing championship golf after they became eligible for the senior tour.

So when I think about what Ben and I accomplished, the line that comes to mind is: In everyone's life there is a "summer of '42." That was our age when I won the U.S. Open and Ben claimed his second Masters.

I doubt if this surprised Harvey; I don't think any of Ben's or my achievements ever did. He knew our parents. He knew what we came from; as he so often reminded us, the apple doesn't fall far from the tree. He knew us over a lot of years, and in many ways he probably knew us better than our parents.

Ben and I talk about Harvey all the time, trying to remember some of his sayings, the encouraging words he gave us. He was a philosopher, and you knew that much of the wisdom he offered came from his own experience. Two of my favorites: A husband should never try to teach his wife to play golf or drive a car; a wife should never try to teach her husband to play bridge.

We think about him every day.

WATER HOLE #3

Entry, August 2, 1937

Jimmy Demaret came up from Houston today and sure shot up our golf course. He had 28-32-60.

I talked to him afterward and he's working on a theory that the elbows should stay together in the swing. He doesn't mean tight together, or in to the body. He just tries to keep them the same distance apart throughout his swing.

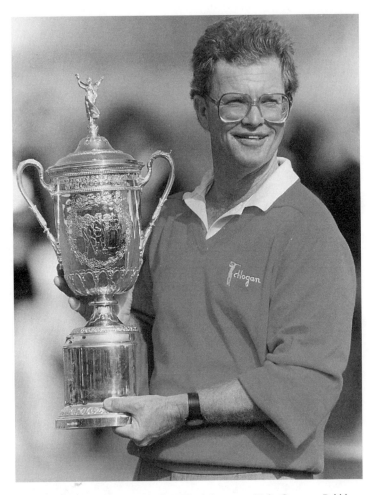

I'm jubilant after winning a big one—the 1992 U.S. Open at Pebble Beach. I won by two strokes over Jeff Sluman.
Reuters/Mike Blake/Archive Photos

Chapter Four

WINNING A
BIG ONE

A magazine writer once described me as golf's version of *The Little Engine That Could*. First I had to prove that I could win on the tour. *Whenever anyone said he couldn't, he just repeated to himself, I know I can, I know I can.*

Then people wondered if I would ever win a major, or win often enough to pull my train to the top of the hill. *He knows he can, he knows he can.*

Hey, I can live with that description. There may be some truth in it. To be honest, I enjoyed hearing that question about not winning a major about as much as I would enjoy classic Japanese opera. I wasn't as mystified as others, including my friend Dan Jenkins, who wrote, "He drives it straight. He invented the third wedge. He's good on fast greens. He knows how to turn three shots into two. He's a smart, patient, methodical player. He comes from Texas. But somehow, [they] keep getting away. . . ."

I began to wonder if the whispers on and off the course that I didn't have what it takes to win the big one were correct. You only get a limited number of chances to compete in a major tournament in a lifetime. If you play twenty years, that is only eighty tournaments, and you may not get in all of them.

If my claim to fame is that no one on the tour out-worked me, so be it. My goal wasn't to be the hardest worker. My goal was to win everything in sight. I was trying to get all I could out of my ability, to do the same thing on Sunday that I did on Thursday, to be as consistent and predictable and as good as possible.

But if hardworking is a euphemism for ungifted, I need to offer a modest dissent. In praising my work ethic, some analysts make it sound as if I had little skill at the game. To paraphrase an old Hungarian proverb, to succeed in the arts it isn't enough to be crazy, one must also have talent. And I consider golf an art. I've always felt good about Tom Kite and his career.

The knocks against me—I didn't hit booming shots off the tee; I had small hands; my vision was a long way from twenty-twenty; I was too cautious, a percentage golfer who cared only for survival—were not meant

All eyes are on the ball: I defeated my friend Davis Love III in a play-off for the 1989 Nestlé Invitational title.

unkindly. On the latter point, the critics could not have been more wrong. It killed me to lose. Still does.

You don't want a steady diet, but an occasional criticism isn't bad. It makes you appreciate things all the more when you turn them around.

By 1982, my tenth year on the tour, I had been on the brink of winning a major so many times that I was more determined than ever to win every time out. That year, I had chipped in for a birdie on the first sudden death hole to win a playoff over Jack Nicklaus and Denis Watson of South Africa.

I lost in the Bob Hope Classic at Palm Springs when Ed Fiori sank a thirty-five-foot putt to beat me. Then I was paired with Jerry Pate in the last round of the Memphis Classic, and Jerry led by a stroke after seventy-one holes.

I had busted a driver and a 3-wood, but I was still forty yards from the green. We both knew I had to get up and down from a bunker to have any hope of forcing a playoff. As we walked up the eighteenth fairway, I was trying to stay focused, and Jerry thought it was over. He had hit a driver and laid up short of the green with a 5-iron.

"You know, Tom," he chattered away, "I could have reached the green easy, I'm so fired up. But I was afraid I'd hit a 4-wood over the TV tower."

Through clenched teeth, I said, "Jerry, you play your game and I'll play mine."

Pate retorted, "Well, get on over in that bunker and play your game, then." Later, he said, "I thought I'd put him away with my mouth, but that son of a gun hit the greatest bunker shot I ever saw. He put it within ten feet of the cup and then he damned near made the putt."

Damned near. That could have been the title for a book. It was the story of my career, up to then.

For twenty years I kept saying it didn't bother me. By

1989 I had become the game's all-time leading money winner, the first pro to earn more than six million dollars. I had been a rookie of the year in 1973 and had won a Bobby Jones award and two Vardon trophies (named after the famed British golfer Harry Vardon and awarded to the player with the lowest scoring average). Going into the 1992 season, I had as many top-ten finishes as just about anybody: over two hundred.

What I didn't have was a major or the kind of validation that comes with one. For almost twenty years I had been saying that if my career had ended at any time in the 1980s, I would have been proud of the record I compiled. I meant every word, but it might not have been the whole truth.

Everything changed on June 23, 1992, a sunny, wind-whipped day on a course loaded with history—Pebble Beach. But I had developed a love affair with this course. When I woke up Sunday morning and stepped outside, I felt the wind and rain in my face. I knew I had a solid chance to win if I took my time and trusted myself.

I relish those days when the wind blows. I dream of days like those; some of my best wins have come in foul weather. It all goes back to when I was a boy. Harvey Penick would encourage us to practice in the worst kind of weather.

While many a top golfer was fighting to keep his game from being blown into the Pacific Ocean, the shots I

Coming out of a trap on the fifth hole during the fourth round of the U.S. Open at Pebble Beach in June 1992: I parred the hole.
Reuters/Blake Sell/Archive Photos

needed to make kept falling into place, and I won the ninety-second U.S. Open. I had waited twenty-one years for that moment, and it was all the sweeter because it happened on Father's Day.

I had scored a kind of family man's clean sweep. My last win had been earlier that year in the BellSouth Classic . . . on Mother's Day. That victory, in Atlanta, had an added importance because it got me to Pebble Beach. Otherwise, I was going to have to qualify in a thirty-six-hole tournament in early June, and those things can be dicey.

Now, finally, I had shed the tag of being The Best Golfer Never to Have Won a Major.

It meant so much more than I can say. I have a great family, and I've had a bountiful career. But in golf there is no substitute for winning.

There is no easy way to explain why it took so long. During a four-year period in the mid-1980s, I was in contention to win in the last round of each of the sport's major tournaments—the Masters, the U.S. Open, the British Open, and the PGA. It didn't happen.

I leave it to Christy to put these things in perspective. "If I had to pick a time that I was most proud of him," she said, "it probably wouldn't be after a win. I've been the proudest when he came back after his disappointments, after he lost the Open in 1989 [a triple bogey in the final round sent me reeling] and the 1984

Christy's victory smile matches my own after I handed her the crystal trophy for winning the 1981 Inverrary Classic.

Masters [when I was leading after three rounds and lost]. After that Masters, he turned around and finished second the next week at Hilton Head. To me, that tells you more about him than a win . . . it's how you handle the disappointments."

Whether we know it or not, each of us has a way of coping with setbacks. Not all ways are good. Some people get into bed and pull the covers over their heads, others eat or drink too much. I try to put it behind me almost immediately. I rely on another Penick admonition: By the time you approach your next shot, be thinking positively. Your next shot is a new experience; it may be the best shot of your life.

Consciously or not, I seldom stepped onto a golf course without Penick-isms in my mind: There is no rush. Swing as if you are working by the hour. Never make a change based on one bad shot, or even a few. If your swing is grooved, you can hit the ball with a sack over your head.

If you are going to persevere, in golf or in anything, you need a philosophy. Harvey gave us one: Stick to the one thing you can control—you. Don't get mad at the club; it's the same one you used to hit that great shot yesterday.

In Pebble Beach on June 23, 1992, I started the fourth round trailing Gil Morgan, who had led after each of the first three rounds, by one stroke. Gil, forty-five, from Oklahoma, had threatened to run away with the tournament. At one point on Saturday he led by seven strokes. But the elements took their toll.

On the first hole, I moved into the lead for the first time, nailing an eighteen-footer for a birdie. Then came a double bogey at Number 4. I got back one stroke with a twenty-footer for a birdie at Number 6, then made one of the best shots ever.

The short seventh hole may have turned the day in

my favor. I tried a 6-iron and the wind blew it well left of the green and in the deep rough. I chose my trusty 62-degree wedge and lobbed a chip shot that was still traveling when it crashed into the pin and fell in. This turned a possible bogey into a birdie for a two-shot swing. I was almost in shock. When it went in, my initial thought was to jump around and run all over the green. But, I still had a lot more holes to play. My calmer instincts took over.

The day was still young, but now I knew the tournament was mine to win—or lose. Pebble Beach made playing far harder Sunday than it had been all week. The weather looked as if it had come out of a movie studio's special effects department and cued the wind machine. To give you an idea of how the wind had changed, I used a sand wedge at Number 7 Saturday. I needed a 6-iron Sunday. You had to fight not only the field, but the tricky, flag-whipping winds gusting up to thirty-five miles an hour, greens drying out so fast they were as hard as cement, and the unsettling presence of the Pacific Ocean, always posing the threat of swallowing shots and sinking hopes. But I felt calm and secure—as I had even when I was eight strokes back after thirty-six holes.

While I was walking up to Number 7, an odd thing happened. Given the conditions, Jack Nicklaus, doing the commentary for television, had decided Colin Montgomerie would win and invited him to the TV booth.

The native of Scotland had teed off two hours ahead of the leaders, avoiding the rougher conditions. He tied for the low round of the day at 70, and was sitting comfortably in the clubhouse, even-par, watching the scores soar and the field coming back to him, when the TV people called.

After he left the booth, Colin told reporters, "Jack said, 'I just want to congratulate you on your first U.S. Open victory.' Immediately after he said that, Tom Kite chipped in."

As the hours passed, the sun tried to peep out from under the clouds, but the blustery winds never quit. It was a very difficult day. The greens were turning blue, then brown. They had gotten tracked up, and some were just treacherous. It was scary.

One by one, the other leaders faltered. Ian Woosnam, the Welshman, skied to a 79. Davis Love struggled in with an 83, Ballesteros a 79. My playing companion, Mark Brooks, a fellow University of Texas ex, would finish with an 84.

Meanwhile, I was staying focused, playing consistently, banishing any negative thoughts. I bogeyed Number 9, but it was a good bogey. My second shot went over the crest of the cliff into the deep weeds, but I managed to find it, then chipped onto the green and two-putted.

I had birdies at Number 12, where I drained a forty-foot putt, and at Number 14, 565 yards long, hitting another pitch to within five feet of the cup. After I made that birdie, I had a lead of four strokes over Jeff Sluman, who was in second place.

On the sixteenth, I missed a short putt that sliced my lead over Sluman to three strokes. On the seventeenth, I hit a great pitch from out of a bunker, only to miss another short putt and get a bogey. Maybe they were not short enough. Harvey would say, "If you're not having success [on the greens], it's because your iron shots are too far from the hole."

My lead over Jeff was down to two strokes heading into Number 18. All of a sudden, I was forced to make a golf swing. I mean, just haul off and have a good rip, forget about doing math in your head or playing safe. The quotable (and conservative) Darrell Royal would call this "letting your skirts fly." Anyone familiar with the gale force winds in Texas, and in Royal's native Oklahoma, knew what he meant: The ladies sometimes had to make a choice between hanging on to their hats or holding their skirts. "Sometimes," Darrell would say, "you just have to let your skirts fly."

As a football fan, I hate the prevent defense, the idea of which, as far as I can see, is to play not to lose. And I'll be darned if in the closing holes I hadn't gone into a prevent defense.

So it was nice to grit up and take a good swing at 18. I had to steady myself for a drive over the water—the

*Celebrating a birdie on the twelfth hole, where I drained a forty-foot putt
during the final round of the U.S. Open at Pebble Beach.*
Reuters/Blake Sell/Archive Photos

biggest water hazard in the world, the Pacific Ocean. That drive was the sweetest shot I hit all day. I didn't relax until after I hit the wedge, my third shot on the par-five finishing hole. It was seventy-three yards, but that is what I had built my game around, a seventy-yard wedge shot. When it landed, I finally gave in to the emotion. I walked up the fairway with my arms raised and saluted the gallery. They were giving me a standing ovation. I lagged the 15-foot putt a couple of inches from the hole, then tapped it in for par and the biggest victory of my career.

I don't think I had ever before heard cheers that loud, directed at me. Fans were cheering their throats raw. It was as if all of them had been waiting with me, twenty years, for this moment.

Only two of us out of the entire field had played sub-par golf. I was three under at 285. Jeff Sluman was one under at 287. Colin Montgomerie, at even par, finished third. Everyone else played over par. Many fine players had to struggle with rounds in the eighties and were making jokes about it.

As I told John Maher, a writer for the Austin newspaper, I felt as though it was my week from the word go, but you never want to say that early on because you can look like a fool if it isn't.

The win came on a course that is legendary for being a true test of champions. It not only came on Father's Day, with nearly all the people I deeply love there to see it, but my parents would celebrate their fiftieth wedding anniversary in a month. My dad tried to be a little blasé about his role in my career: "I'm happy for Tom," he said, "but it was only coincidental that it came on Father's Day."

He was right about that—I have no control over the calendar. But my mom, Mauryene, squealed on him: "It absolutely thrilled him. He has dreamed of Tom winning the U.S. Open for a long time."

There is one untold story about that day. My father had flown to California carrying a putter at his side, one I had asked him to bring. It had no magical powers, but it was a putter I liked, especially when the greens were fast, and I had failed to bring it with me. I used it all week.

How bad was the weather? Everyone complained, but I liked what Richard Zokol said, after going even par for three days and then shooting an 80 in the last round. "It's the U.S. Open," he said. "This is what it's all about, dealing with adversity. A lot of the pros are spoiled. Hey, there's nothing wrong with going eighteen rounds with Godzilla and losing."

I've done both, and winning is better.

My dad had lived through all my wins and losses with me. He now recalled the 1989 Open, at Oak Hills in Rochester, New York, when I led by three shots with fourteen holes to play. I double-bogeyed the fifth hole, finished with a 78, and watched Curtis Strange walk away with the victory. Dad was at his home in Austin that day, watching the Rochester Open on television along with Mr. Penick and a crew from ABC. Dad hadn't wanted the TV people there, but they persisted, and he agreed.

"It was just awful," he said. "I'd never do it again. Here I am watching Tom blow a three-shot lead on one hole. You can't express your emotions in front of the press. You don't want to talk."

I knew that feeling. You have to force a smile. Your face feels as if it will crack. As I worked on protecting my lead at Pebble Beach, I tried not to think of the time I'd had a similar lead, at Oak Hills. I found out that Dad was doing the same thing. "It was in the back of my mind," he admitted. "It crossed Tom's, too, but he put it out. I felt good about the way he was playing this time. I didn't have the uneasy feeling I had at Oak Hills, although with the wind at Pebble Beach, one shot is all it takes for a triple bogey."

He's a proud and stubborn guy, my father. Dad wouldn't concede that I had broken a twenty-one-year drought. "Tom and I both feel that any golf tournament you win is a major," he said. "I felt he won a major when he won the Players Championship [in 1989]. It was the strongest field in golf. He won the Western Open [in 1986], which used to be a major. But it's hard to get people to see it differently."

Dad had a point, and I agreed with him, but one tends to let go of traditions slowly, if at all. In the heyday of Bobby Jones, the grand slam included the U.S. and British Amateurs. Today the slam consists of the U.S. and British Opens, the Masters, and the PGA Championship.

The majors are what they are. A lot of very good golfers never win one. Then you have someone like Andy North, who won two U.S. Opens and only one other event. At times, neither hard work nor talent is enough. It's up to the vagaries of fate.

Speaking of which, my dad reminisced that day about how he had tried to discourage me from turning pro. "I thought he should be an architect or an engineer," he told the media at Pebble Beach. "He has the aptitude for those. The odds of becoming a pro golfer are really poor. Every year about two thousand people try to get their cards. Only about fifty do, and over half of them lose the cards the first year."

Sometimes you just have to beat the odds.

Christy was at my side that day by the Pacific, and I could see the tears silently streaking her face as I accepted the trophy for the 1992 U.S. Open. I can't express the exhilaration I felt, and I wondered how Harvey was reacting. I knew his eyeballs would be virtually plugged into the TV set.

Back in Austin, the telephone was getting a strenuous workout at the home of Harvey Penick. With Har-

*As good as winning the 1992 U.S. Open was the kiss I got from my wife,
Christy.* Reuters/Blake Sell/Archive Photos

vey's hearing so weak, Helen Penick took the calls and relayed his answers. They were from friends and writers, my well-wishers and his, just wanting to know how he felt.

"We watched every minute of it," Helen kept telling them. "Harvey is very proud and very emotional. He thought Tom was going to win this year. He was very tense watching it. He knew how dangerous the course was."

There was a buzz in the media. On television, Jack Nicklaus had been talking about Harvey, and our relationship, as I was finishing the final round.

"That was a very big thrill for Harvey," said Helen.

Mark Rosner, a columnist for the *American-Statesman*, called most of the population of Austin, or so it seemed, to get their reactions. One was my former college teammate, Brent Buckman, by then the director of golf at Barton Creek Country Club. "Watching him walk up 18, I just felt for him," said Brent. "It's great to see a guy who works so hard reach his dream."

Buckman offered what I thought was a nice insight. "Tom is always real focused. I talked to him about a month ago, and he didn't talk about how badly he wanted to win the Open. He doesn't talk about stuff like that. But you could tell.

"When he failed to qualify for the [1992] Masters, he wouldn't discuss it. That was the past. He wanted to think about the future. Not qualifying for the Masters may have been the best thing that happened to him. He became more driven, more focused than ever."

Emotions ran deep. George Hannon, my college coach at Texas who had succeeded Mr. Penick, was quoted as saying he cried when I won. Harvey went even further: Sitting in front of his TV set, he said that when they put the trophy in my hands "my toes curled up and I cried like a baby."

Harvey wasn't one of those people who wept at the sight of an empty gum wrapper. But when a moment had been so many years in the making and involved someone he cared about, the water works opened up.

A couple of years later, I came close to tears myself, when I thumbed through a copy of his *Little Green Book* and came upon the passage where he described my victory at Pebble Beach as "one of the finest, most courageous rounds of golf in the history of the game."

My only regret was that I wouldn't be returning to Austin after the Open. I had an outing scheduled in St. Louis the next day, and from there would fly on to Westchester for the Buick Classic. Christy flew to St. Louis with me before flying home Monday night. I asked her to take the trophy to the club, first thing Tuesday morning, and present it to Harvey. My exact words were "Put it right in his lap."

When she spotted him, he was in his golf cart, giving a lesson to a woman from Rhode Island. Christy walked up to him and said, "Mr. Penick, this is for you." Then she put the U.S. Open trophy right in his lap.

That was pretty neat.

Harvey cried. Then Christy started. Then everybody who saw them and realized what was going on started laughing and bawling. It is a rare time when people are so happy they can cry.

Texas is a feast or famine state. We have periods of drought and scalding heat that kill the grass the cattle need to live. In other years, floods wash away the crops and some of the stock. Either way, the farmers and ranchers struggle to survive. Maybe this has something to do with why strong people are able to let their emotions hang out.

Another week went by before I could take a break from the tour and visit with Harvey. When at last we met, he asked what I was thinking when I battled those horrible weather conditions. I had just the right answer for him.

"I was thinking, 'Take your time.' "

He gave a quick hand-clap and said, "Tell me about it."

Harvey had always impressed on us not to hurry if we were being buffeted by cold or winds or rain. I said, "With players being blown away, you have to forget about your swing or any mechanical thoughts and get

Giving in to emotion after sinking the winning putt at the 1992 U.S. Open:
I tapped it in for par and the biggest victory of my life.

into a mentality where you really trust your instincts."
This goes back to my decision to "swing away" on the
last holes. I recalled another of Harvey's lessons: The
ability to concentrate is good, but thinking too much
about *how* you are doing *what* you are doing can be dis-
astrous.

You just have to take the attitude that you've done all
the training that is required, and what is the point of that
training if you're not going to trust it? That was a favorite
phrase of Bob Rotella, the sports psychologist who had
worked with me. Harvey liked it.

"I use that thought an awful lot," I told Harvey, "when
I'm on the golf course and I have a chance to win. I keep
telling myself to trust it, just go ahead and trust it.

"As for taking my time, I mean I want to be totally
ready to play before I play the shot . . . in bad weather,
if it takes a little longer to get ready, then I need to take
a little longer."

You could see his eyes light up. To Harvey, this was
another way of saying I had taken "dead aim."

There was at least one other footnote to my first major
championship. I putted cross-handed. I had experimented
with this grip off and on since 1989, and had used it
when I won the St. Jude Classic in 1990 and the Tournament of Champions in 1991. I had been struggling to
regain my putting touch before the 1992 Open, and this
was an option, but one that attracted some snickering
from the other pros, the media, and fans.

It was a grip for six-year-olds or for those over the hill, or so the critics thought. "He putted well cross-handed," Christy defended me, "but he caught so much grief for it. To many golfers, putting cross-handed is a last-ditch thing. You putt cross-handed before you die."

For me, it was a way to redirect some of my attention onto my short game. That is really what I built my career on and what enabled me to play consistently for so long.

They don't give style points in golf. The main thing Harvey got across to Ben and me was how to score. He taught us that the object of the game is numbers, not looking pretty. What's best is what works.

In fact, Harvey had no problem with the cross-handed grip for chipping or putting. (Obviously, when you drive, you are going to hit a ball farther with a conventional grip.) "But I would suggest that anyone should try it," he said. "The left wrist stays firm automatically with a cross-handed chip or putt.

"The first time most children pick up a club and swing it," he notes, "they do so cross-handed. . . . Instinctively, a [right-handed] child knows that to hit a ball with a golf club, the left arm must be straight at impact. Pick up a club and try a slow cross-handed swing and you'll see what I mean."

I'm not being defensive—at least, I try not to be. But go back and compare Sam Snead and Ben Hogan, two of the game's icons. Hogan would never, ever putt cross-handed or sidesaddle or croquet style.

It was several weeks after the 1992 U.S. Open before I could take a break
from the tour and visit Harvey. Tinsley joined in the reunion.
Copyright © by Carrell Grigsby

But Ben Hogan was no longer competitive in his fif-
ties, and Sam was. Sam made the adjustments he
needed to make to be able to compete. If that meant
putting croquet-style, he did. When they outlawed
that, he went sidesaddle. To me, that is what the game
is all about, finding a way that allows you to play your
best.

Hogan was less likely to adjust, but in fairness he
didn't have Sam's health. He had cheated death in a terrible car crash in his prime.

I never second-guess or criticize people for doing what
they think can help them become the best they can be.

If I feel like putting cross-handed or standing on my head, I won't hesitate to do it—within the rules of the game.

For one fine week in 1992 at Pebble Beach, I didn't need any special favors, any four-leaf clovers, any prayers to the weather gods. As so many headline writers noted, it was just an ideal week for a high-flyin' Kite.

WATER HOLE #4

The worst trouble pupils have is that they try to think of the thousand and one things they hear. We all have to check our mistakes, but it's impossible to go through the list before each stroke.

It's so important not to give up a golf swing in an effort to do some minor or inconsequential thing. I've seen a lot of players with a good straight left arm. Trouble is, they gave up their golf swings to do it.

A victorious 1993 U.S. Ryder Cup team with the trophy at The Belfry Golf Club in Sutton Coldfield, England. Starting at rear from left: John Cook, Raymond Floyd, Lanny Wadkins, Corey Pavin, Lee Janzen, and Payne Stewart. Tom Watson is in the middle, and I'm kneeling in the foreground in front of Chip Beck.
AP/Wide World Photos

Chapter Five

THE RYDER CUP

I played in my first of seven Ryder Cups in 1979 and, as Raymond Floyd once put it, "If you haven't played in one before, you can't hardly get through it the first time."

He was, and is, right. There is nothing that prepares you for this epic battle. When the Cup is played in Europe, you arrive a week or two ahead of time, and even in practice you're nervous. You might have fun and even pranks with your teammates, but when you tee off on Friday you and your partner are going against two other guys, and the fans from both sides are screaming and cheering. It is a totally different feeling from any other event in golf.

You have to understand the unique character of the Ryder Cup. It isn't the Masters or the U.S. or British

Opens, yet it has a touch of them all. It is part Olympics—the Dream Team leaps to mind—and part Harvard versus Oxford at Henley. The name itself evokes flags and a carousel and hands across the sea, if not leather boots and polo ponies.

Every other golf tournament is about fame and money. This one is primarily about honor and country and teamwork. It is the most intense competition that any golfer will ever experience. Once you have played in the Ryder Cup, everything else becomes less difficult.

On the tour, each of us is self-employed, an individual contractor. You play only for yourself and your family, and if you lose it doesn't bother anyone else—in fact, it may please a few. Now, all of a sudden, you are representing the United States of America. And, hoo boy, you can get chills thinking about it. When you stand out there and they raise the flag and they play "The Star-Spangled Banner," you get goose bumps.

In the Masters, on the last day you feel the tension when you're near the lead. In the Ryder Cup, whether it's the first day or the third, the first hole or the eighteenth green, your stomach never stops churning. You feel as if squirrels are running around inside you. Anyone who tells you they competed in the Ryder Cup and felt no nervousness is lying.

I received a call in October 1996—telling me that Jim Awtrey, the executive director of the PGA, was planning

to be in Austin. He invited me to meet him for breakfast
at his hotel if I was in town. I was and we met. There
had been rumors that I was under consideration as Ryder
Cup captain, but nothing had been said on the phone to
make me think, "Whoa, this could be Ryder Cup stuff."
It could have been anything.

When you have played in a few Ryder Cups, the
thought is in the back of your mind that it would be
nice, someday, to be named the captain of the team.
There is no campaigning for the job and no negotiation.
Jim said the PGA board had voted to offer me the cap-
taincy, if I wanted to take it on, and I assured him I did.
I can't imagine that anyone ever declined.

It didn't occur to me to ask, why me, or who else was
considered? I am not even sure of the criteria. Obviously,
you need to have played a lot of good golf over a period
of years and to have been a member of the team, won a
major championship, conducted yourself in a manner the
PGA would deem beneficial to the game, and shown that
you can get along with other players and the press. The
list gets fairly short right there.

I don't believe you have to fit any specific profile in
terms of personality. The captains have run the gamut.
It would be nice, of course, if you could blend the dignity
of Hogan, the humor of Trevino, the concentration of
Nicklaus, and the outgoing nature of Dave Marr.

When I accepted, I made up my mind I was not going

A great honor! PGA president Tom Addis III congratulates me on being named captain of the 1997 U.S. Ryder Cup team, at PGA headquarters in Palm Beach Gardens, Florida. AP/Wide World Photos

to get caught up in the speculation over which players were likely to end up on the twelve-man team. The top ten scorers, based on their finishes in events sanctioned by the PGA Tour between January 1996 and August 1997 would be invited; as captain, I would get to pick the final two players.

While the PGA staff handles the travel arrangements, the captain's list isn't short: He approves the logo and the color schemes and the luggage, and he picks the suppliers, from the artist who paints the team poster to the company that makes the team gift. I carry a laptop computer with me on planes and in hotel rooms, type in my letters and notes and memos, and overnight the disks to Christy to be printed. The system works fine.

As this is written, the Cup is still several months away. The advantage is with the reader. Depending on when you read this book, you may know the shape of decisions as yet unmade, and who my two captain's choices are, and even the outcome of the matches.

Still, it might be amusing—for you, not me—to compare what I write here to what occurs in Sotogrande, Spain, the last week in September of 1997.

I went into the year hopeful that America's team would include a playing captain. I was well aware of the burdens and the odds. To begin with, I have to pull my game out of a ditch. If I am going to play for Captain Tom, it will have to be on merit, not mercy. But there isn't much

*Seve Ballesteros, 1997 European Ryder Cup team captain, laughingly
snatches the Ryder Cup trophy away after a joint news conference on
October 9, 1996. Ballesteros and I both will be first-time captains in 1997.*
Reuters/Enrique Shore/Archive Photos

that motivates me more than a task that looks as if it
can't be done.

The challenge is all the more interesting, knowing that
my counterpart will be Seve Ballesteros, someone I admire and enjoy. I have a hunch he might be going
through the same mental processing.

There hasn't been a playing captain for the United
States since Arnold Palmer in 1963, when the United
States won in a cakewalk, 23 to 9, at the East Lake Coun-

try Club. Arnie won one and lost one in singles play, won one and lost one in foursomes, and was 2-for-2 in four-balls. Before 1977, they played an afternoon singles match.

The last captain for the European team, at that time the British, was Dai Rees in 1961. The United States won in a tighter match, 14½ to 9½, with Rees taking both of his singles matches and getting a split in the foursomes.

As this is written, it is a huge guessing game. Part of me says, Yeah, I still want to be a player. The other part says, I'm the captain and I'll have plenty on my plate; I don't need to be worrying about my game when I'll have a lot of tough decisions to make. It helps that I am an organized person. What needs to be done will get done. Nothing will be left to the last minute.

I will get plenty of advice, of course, as to whether I should or should not play: a jillion opinions in every newspaper and magazine that covers golf, and more from the fans. Nothing that is said or written will put pressure on me. If I haven't played well during the year, the question is a moot point. It is entirely up to me to become the player I was in 1992 and 1993. If I *made* the twelve-man roster, I still might not choose to play. It would depend on where I finished in the rankings. If I am in the top five, I don't think there would be many players who would help the team more.

On the other hand, if I squeezed in under the wire,

and I knew another player could do as well, my instinct would tell me, *Don't play*, concentrate on being the captain.

By mid-May, only one player had reached the 800-point level and made the team—Tiger Woods. I find it more than a little amazing that he did this in his first seven months on the tour. I'm pleased to have him, and I will throw out two predictions right now: Tiger will play brilliantly, and he will have the time of his life.

He is going to get closer to a group of golfers than he ever has. He will form a bond that will last as long as his career. And he will learn from his new friends in ways he never expected.

This doesn't mean he makes my job any softer. For this one week every two years, golf is a team game. And Tiger will be reminded, as we all are, that teamwork means making personal sacrifices and putting the team first. The media and the galleries are going to swamp him, clamor for him, love-bomb him even more than they already have. I don't see how we can hide him. It will be a test of his maturity—and ours. He has passed a bunch of tests so far. My guess is that he will handle this one, too.

When Tiger first turned pro, I tried to withhold judgment until I could learn more about him: What motivated him, how would he deal with the public and the press, was he introspective, who were his role models, how

Nick Faldo, winner of the 1996 Masters, helps 1997 winner, Tiger Woods, with his green jacket. Woods will play on the U.S. Ryder Cup team for the first time in 1997, and it will be a great experience for all of us.
Copyright © by PGA Tour/Sam Greenwood

would he deal with his early success, and, of more importance, how would he handle himself when bad breaks or bad times struck?

At the rate he is going, we may all be old and gumming our food before we find the answer to that last question. I have seen enough to make me a fan of Tiger Woods. I saw him from twelve strokes back, as he won the first major he ever played in, the 1997 Masters, and I finished second—a very quiet second, but one that gave my morale a kickstart.

I was playing well and could feel my game taking off, edging close to my form of 1992 and early 1993. Of course, no one was playing as well as Tiger, who just blew the course away. It wasn't just that his shots were so long and so true; the precision of his play and his movements all said, *I take this work seriously.*

What can anyone say about this twenty-one-year-old, ex–Stanford student who can top these numbers: 270, the lowest score in Masters history, breaking the record held by Nicklaus; eighteen under par; in his first sixteen starts—four wins, one second, two thirds.

I was cautious, not skeptical, when he left the campus to join the tour. In sports or show business, there always seems to be a flavor of the month. Athletes come out of nowhere to dazzle us for a game or a season, then disappear. You get to know and judge greatness only over time.

Besides, I can remember the mania that greeted the debut of Nicklaus. Others may have forgotten that Ben Crenshaw broke in like a sunburst, winning his first tourney, the Texas Open, finishing second two weeks later in the World Open. Nicklaus went on to become an icon, and Ben was a shooting star, but Tiger Woods . . . well, we may have to invent new words to describe him.

I am excited about the impact he will have on the game, on the young players and new fans he can bring to it, the records he will threaten, and the good will he has a chance to generate here and abroad.

*My partner, an overjoyed Calvin Peete (right), embraces me after we
beat Bernhard Langer (left) of Germany and Nick Faldo of England
at the 1985 Ryder Cup in Sutton Coldfield, England.*
AP/Wide World Photos

There is always the risk that he will be overexposed
and resented by those who think that no one deserves
to have it all. He may burn out trying to reenter Earth's
atmosphere, or the Elvis-type treatment may spoil or en-
gulf him. But I doubt it. His parents deserve credit for
how wisely they prepared him for this moment.

Among his records, he will be the youngest golfer ever
to compete in the Ryder Cup. He makes my hand as the
captain stronger; I imagine it would be even more interesting to be Tiger's teammate.

Whether I play or not, my eighth Ryder Cup will tie

the number of appearances by Raymond Floyd and Lanny Wadkins. In each of my other seven, I came away with even greater respect for the Cup and the kinship, not only with my teammates but with my European opponents. My Ryder Cup record is fifteen wins, nine losses, two ties.

The strongest argument for my playing is this: It would mean I was at the top of my game again, once more among the best dozen or so players on the tour. A distinction needs to be made: The two wild card picks do not have to be the next highest on the scoring or money lists; they need to be the best for the Ryder Cup competition.

But I can tell you, it is a fine line we all walk that week. In 1989, Floyd was captain, and he had to caution Freddie Couples against his Mr. Nice Guy routine and his habit of telling a foe "Nice shot" or "Great going." "You can be friends with them another time," Ray lectured him. "For one week, we're trying to beat these guys."

Naturally, no one feels the weight of trying to win more than the captain does. In 1967, the Ryder Cup was held at Champions in Houston, and the captain was Ben Hogan. The Hawk brought to the job the same intensity he felt as a player. When Doug Sanders and Gay Brewer lost their Friday morning match to Tony Jacklin and Dave Thomas, Ben dropped them from the afternoon lineup.

"Hogan," cracked Bobby Nichols, a member of that team, "is like Bear Bryant. If you don't win the first time, he won't risk losing twice with the same personnel."

Of course, the Ryder Cup back then was not the Ryder Cup we know today. The event wasn't in much demand in the early 1980s, when the PGA of America and the PGA Tour (the two major bodies governing the Cup) decided who would run what. The PGA of America, the club pros, wound up managing the Ryder Cup.

The history of the event dates back to 1926, when Samuel Ryder, a wealthy British seed merchant and a patron of golf, offered to put up a solid gold trophy for a series of matches between professionals of his nation and ours. America won the first Ryder Cup match ever held, in 1927, and twenty-one of the next twenty-five, with one tie. The rivalry didn't really exist. The British simply couldn't match the size of the purses and the quality of the golfers who chased them in the States. You had to be a really devout golf fan to care how the scores turned out, and the media on both sides of the ocean greeted it with a yawn.

Then, in 1979, interest in the Ryder Cup was revived, and it became a true contest, when the best of Europe—including the United Kingdom—replaced the team from Great Britain and Ireland. Ever since then, it has been the golfing event of the year. As Raymond Floyd said, "I no longer refer to it as a tournament, it's a spectacle."

No one can say that Floyd didn't go out on a high

We wore our flag pins proudly in our lapels, but Tom Watson (center),
Lanny Wadkins, and I were not smiling after the 1989 Ryder Cup ended
in a tie.

note. In 1993, as a captain's pick by Tom Watson, he
sank the putt that beat Spain's José María Olazabal to
win the Cup. In 1991, Floyd had played on the U.S. team
that took back the Cup after an absence of six years.
Dave Stockton was the captain.

There is a story following Floyd around that reveals a
glimpse of the grip the Ryder Cup has on those who
play in it. I played on the team he captained in 1989,
when the matches ended in a tie and Europe kept the
trophy. Fred Couples missed a putt that cost him not

only his match with the Irish player Christy O'Connor, Jr., but in his mind the Cup as well. Under the rules, in the event of a tie the team that last won the Cup retains possession.

Raymond dropped by Freddie's hotel room later that day. He found him in a tearful fog. "He was hurting terribly," recalled Ray. "I told him, 'Look, we're a team. This wasn't one man's doing. Believe me, I speak from experience, you have just jumped a hurdle. You are now going to go on to the next level. You will win a major. The Ryder Cup does that.' "

Floyd, the old warhorse, could hardly have imagined how quickly Couples would make him a prophet. He may have been simply trying to lift the spirits of a wounded buddy, but I suspect he meant exactly what he said. Ray is known for his candor, not his diplomacy. After Floyd's pep talk, Fred went on to win eight titles in the next five years, including his first major. He won the 1992 Masters, edging out Corey Pavin and—who else? Ray Floyd.

"That was bizarre," said Couples. "I've got my best buddy playing good and I figure, hey, if I don't win it he will. This is really a tacky way to look at it, but on the other hand I thought it would be great to beat a player of his caliber, a guy who helped me so much."

In the Ryder Cup, players are thrown together for a short, intense time, and for better or worse you share the joy or the despair. The Ryder Cups I played in were all special, and they evoke lots of memories. Part of the experience is getting to know your twelve teammates— and the thirteen on the other side—much better.

Match play is an ancient and different game that still baffles Americans. What they find confusing is that in the Ryder Cup matches (unlike a basic tour event), individual scores don't matter. It's every match that is vital, each worth one point. Win or lose, every player puts his head on his pillow after the final day, knowing he will have a story to tell.

I made every team from 1979 through 1989, missed a turn in 1991, and came back in 1993. Bill Casper was my first captain at Greenbrier in White Sulphur Springs in 1979, which happened to be a U.S. team's first encounter with Team Europe. We won fairly handily, and Casper proved to be a good captain, although he wrestled with things that didn't always bother the golfers. I beat Tony Jacklin in my first individual match and teamed with Hale Irwin to trump Tim Brown and Doug Smith 7-and-6, as bad a beating as their side had ever suffered in four-ball.

The 1981 team that traveled to Walton Heath in Surrey, England, is the one the historians call the best ever assembled—Jack Nicklaus, Tom Watson, Johnny Miller, Lee Trevino, Ray Floyd, Ben Crenshaw, Bruce Lietzke, Hale Irwin, Bill Rogers, Larry Nelson, Jerry Pate, and me. For me to play Sandy Lyle in the finals was a personal

Lining up the putt of teammate Curtis Strange during the opening round of the 1989 Ryder Cup in Sutton Coldfield, England
Reuters/David Brauchli/Archive Photos

highlight. I won 3-and-2, finishing ten under par and Sandy eight under—just spectacular golf. It was the last time the U.S. team would dominate the matches, 18½ to 9½.

I played under Nicklaus twice, winning at West Palm Beach in 1983 and losing at Muirfield Village in Ohio in 1987. That loss was a double insult because it took place in Jack's hometown. Nicklaus was as organized and businesslike as usual. I thought we were just outgunned that year. The Fab Five was cooking for Europe: Nick Faldo, Seve Ballesteros, Bernhard Langer, Ian Woosnam, and José María Olazabal. They were from England, Germany, Spain, and Wales, and between them they would win the Masters eight times.

I played at The Belfry in Sutton Coldfield, one of England's historic courses, in 1985, 1989, and 1993, each a journey into the past but a good walk spoiled when we lost the first and tied the second. I had great individual matches with Ballesteros (1985) and Bernhard Langer (1993). I halved the match with Seve and defeated Langer 5-and-3. My partners were Davis Love III, Larry Nelson, Calvin Peete, and Hale Irwin. Tom Watson was our captain when we won on our third trip to Sutton Coldfield.

It seems to be true, as the press kept arguing, that in 1989 the Europeans had the better mix. They had been poor and unknown together. Now they were rich and

Christy (in her official wives' blazer) and I get our turn to cradle the Ryder Cup trophy at the opening ceremonies in 1993; the United States staged a stirring comeback to beat Europe, 15 to 13, at The Belfry.

famous together. They had won together (in 1985 and 1987 with virtually the same lineup). Going into the match, the Americans were viewed as a cluster of all-stars. If all-stars don't hit home runs, they're in trouble.

But our group had more team spirit than I had seen

before, and we rooted hard for one another in 1989. The pressure on the U.S. team boiled down to this: We had won so often that losing was no longer acceptable. That year's tie simply magnified our frustration.

"We've forgotten how to win," said Nicklaus, the 1987 captain, "because we have it too easy on our tour." He meant the elegant courses, fancy hotels, courtesy cars, and the pampering players now took for granted.

Although neither team won, the 1989 Cup was among the most dramatic of all. On Sunday I got hot, had seven birdies in the first eleven holes, and beat Howard Clark for our first point. Chip Beck beat Langer to become the only unbeaten American. Paul Azinger sneaked out a gutsy win over Ballesteros, and Lanny Wadkins defeated Nick Faldo.

That should have been enough, but it wasn't. The eighteenth hole, a par 4, a dogleg left that demanded a long tee shot over water and then a brave carry over another stretch of water, sometimes into the wind, decided the match. Payne Stewart and Mark Calcavecchia drove into the lake on 18 and lost their matches.

So the overall contest ended in a tie that felt like a loss. With the caliber of our players, I thought we should have won. But if you can't keep the ball out of the water, you usually don't.

The grandstand quarterbacks gave Floyd hell after the first morning, when we gained a 3-to-1 lead in foursomes.

He broke up the teams, Curtis Strange and me, Wadkins and Stewart, and we were blanked in the afternoon four-balls.

Raymond's motives were pure. "I've got twelve players on my team," he said, "and I wanted to give everyone a chance to play every day." Almost in unison, the American press corps retorted: "We didn't know it was Little League. We thought we came over here to win the Cup."

So anyone who sticks his neck out and takes on the role of Ryder Cup captain knows he is going to catch some heat. Even the golf courses get second-guessed. Some of our media described The Belfry as a dressed-up potato field. The fact is, almost every golf course in the U.K. and Europe, and a few in America, was once a marsh or a shepherd's meadow or even a potato field.

The U.S. won the next time around, in 1991. I wasn't picked for the squad that recovered the Cup that year, but I was playing the best golf of my life when the teams were assembled two years later. We were back at The Belfry with Watson as captain, and we all gained some redemption. He did a meticulous job, and we won it by two points.

We were down by a point after the two days of the 1993 series but then won it with a rousing comeback, winning six singles matches and halving two others. It was a squeaker, 15 to 13, as Ray Floyd, at fifty-one the oldest player in Ryder Cup history, sank three birdie putts on the third day to clinch it. That was the year I beat Langer.

By 1995, I was on the sidelines again, struggling to rediscover that winning touch. I could only ache from a distance for my friend Lanny Wadkins, who was roundly faulted by the critics for using his captain's picks on Curtis Strange and Fred Couples. Curtis hadn't won on the tour since 1989; Couples had been nursing a sore back.

Couples managed to halve his match with a scrambling par against Ian Woosnam on Sunday, but Curtis couldn't save par on any of the last three holes, and Europe won by a point. It was a heartwarming win for their captain, Bernard Gallacher, who had been on the losing side in ten straight Ryder Cups, eight as a player and two as a captain. But I don't think Lanny Wadkins doubted himself at all about picking Curtis and Fred. I'm proud of the way he stood by his players and his convictions.

Now the scene, and the tradition, and the pressure have shifted to Valderamma Golf Club in scenic Sotogrande, on Spain's Costa del Sol. The thirty-second Ryder Cup will have been the first to be held in a European country other than England or Scotland. The original course was laid out by Robert Trent Jones, Sr., in 1974 and redesigned by him in 1985. For nearly a decade the course has been the site of the final European PGA event, the Volvo Masters.

Tom Watson, captain of the 1993 U.S. Ryder Cup team, gives pointers to President Clinton at the White House, September 20, 1993. From left: Watson, Chip Beck, John Cook, Raymond Floyd, President Clinton, me, and Corey Pavin. AP/Wide World Photos

The seventh and eleventh holes offer a panoramic view of the Mediterranean Sea, a distraction for the golfers but a bonus for the gallery. The course lies a few miles north of Gibraltar. With its vast bunkers, coastal breezes, and an abundance of cork and olive trees (five hundred), there are plenty of ways to go wrong.

While the Spanish are famous for their hospitality, I am more concerned with the competition Seve Ballesteros and his European players will provide. How we respond is at least partly up to me. My goal is to give the team everything it needs and not shy away from making a tough call.

Among the first advice I received was to not make the mistakes others have made. If the history of the Ryder Cup has taught me anything, it is this: Decisions are only mistakes if they turn out badly.

WATER HOLE #5

Entry, October 15, 1946

There was a young girl from the university who came to me for a lesson today. She wore blue jeans and a bad grip. I've never seen a better, though unpolished, prospect.

Betsy Rawls is quite shy. I'm not too wordy either, so little was said during the lesson. But I don't think she'll need much talking to. If she can get some breaks, and some time from her studies, there's no telling how far she might go.

*Harvey and Ben at the Austin Country Club in February 1994 during the
filming of an NBC-TV special* Gary Edwards

Chapter Six

A QUIET GOOD-BYE

I don't know the chronology of all of Harvey's surgeries, or the extent of the pain from his various ailments. Maybe nobody does. I just know that we kept preparing ourselves to lose him and always he rallied.

In 1991, he was in the hospital to be treated for bleeding ulcers and, as long as he was there, he underwent surgery for prostate cancer. His family wondered if, at his age, there was any point in putting him through this ordeal.

The doctor said, "If it was my father, I would." His son, Tinsley, made the decision: "Then let's do it."

Harvey was then eighty-six, a Joblike figure, hooked up to an oxygen tank. Tubes appeared to be dripping fluids and painkillers into every part of his wasted body. Oh, he was hurting. When Christy and I left the hospital the first day, we were convinced we had seen him alive for the last time. I cried a lot that night. But he pulled through.

We visited him nearly every day, and we left each time feeling the same way, but he defied the medical wisdom, the odds, and logic. After a month in the hospital, he improved enough to go home. He didn't exactly rebuild his strength, but his will to live remained. His mind was as lucid and sharp as ever.

After miraculously surviving that 1991 illness, with Bud Shrake's help he published *The Little Red Book*, and just working on the book revitalized him. It gave him a reason to look ahead, to live; it gave him a shot of adrenalin that kept him going, enabling him to add probably three or four really solid years to his life.

"When I first told my agent about the idea," recalled Shrake, "she said, 'That book won't sell two copies.' People would fall down and roll around on the floor when I said this, but I expected it to sell a million."

Even Helen Penick had taken a minimal view. "I knew it would sell a thousand," she says, "because the members of the Austin Country Club would buy that many. They wouldn't want Harvey to be embarrassed."

At last count, the book had sold one million, eight hundred thousand copies. No golf book in the history of publishing had come close to producing even half those numbers. At last, Harvey Penick was a household name. He had more money than he had ever imagined. As late as all of it came, the timing wasn't a loss. The fame was pleasant, and the money made him comfortable, not just in a material way, but in knowing that all of Helen's needs would be met, and those of his children and grandchildren and Penicks as yet unborn.

There is a charming story behind the birth of the book. Harvey had jotted down his ideas, his impressions, and his advice over a period of sixty years. He kept them in a red Scribbletex notebook, adding pages as he went along, never making another copy. He never intended to have it published; he doubted there would be any interest in his doing so, nor would he want to appear to be promoting himself.

His only thought was to give it eventually to his son, Tinsley, the only other person to read what he had always called his "little red book." Not even Helen had, but she lived a lot of it and heard most of the rest.

Although several of his star pupils asked, he declined to show it to them, "no matter how much I loved them," he wrote. He preferred to tell them personally what they needed to know to help their game. He wasn't sure the rest of his notebook would interest them. His writings were meant to help Tinsley become a better teacher.

Then in the spring of 1991, he was sitting in his golf

cart under the trees at the Austin Country Club, attended by his nurse, when Bud Shrake stopped by to say hello. Bud is a writer and novelist whose older brother, Bruce, had played on one of Harvey's University of Texas golf teams.

They talked, and Harvey made a rare, impulsive decision. He unlocked his briefcase and handed Bud the only copy of his notebook. He asked him if he would help him "get it in shape" to be published. Tinsley came out of the clubhouse to join them. He had always wanted his father to share that wealth of information and logic.

Not long after that meeting under the trees, Bud Shrake stopped by Harvey's house to tell him they had a contract from a publisher for $90,000. According to Bud, Harvey's face fell and he said, "I don't think I can afford that kind of money." Had anyone else said it, you might have thought it was a joke. But Shrake cheerfully explained that the publisher was paying him, not the other way around.

Shrake's agent had changed her mind after seeing samples of Harvey's gospel, his wit and wisdom.

The book's success went well beyond the endorsement of so many top players and teachers. I think it reflected an appreciation for the clarity of his advice, the simplicity of his lessons on life. As I said earlier, it struck the same chord as the book and movie about Forrest Gump.

It was uncanny to see Harvey bounce back, even as

*In the early 1990s Mr. Penick's favorite pastime was to park his golf cart
in the shade under the trees and watch the action on the course unfold.
Here he is with his co-author, Bud Shrake.*

Copyright © by Carrell Grigsby

Ben and I participated in the filming of the videos for Harvey's first two books. Those times turned out to be among the best experiences in our lives and revitalized Harvey after his 1991 illness.
Courtesy of Tinsley Penick

he watched Ben and me participate in the video of *Harvey Penick's Little Red Book*. We weren't shown together; Ben would demonstrate a certain shot in one scene, and I would do a different shot in another scene.

Then he asked us to help make the video for Harvey Penick's *Little Green Book*, in which we'd all work together, with Harvey coaching the two of us. Ben and I both groaned when we discussed doing these tapes because we had a real concern about whether Harvey could handle the workload. We'd already seen a pile of books as high as his shoulder, waiting by his chair to be autographed. The cycle was clear: The more books and tapes that were sold, the more attention he'd get and the more he'd be asked to sign. Was that a good thing for him? You might love ice cream, but you don't want it shoveled down your throat by the gallon.

Of course, Harvey didn't share any of our doubts. He persuaded us to do the tapes, and we're glad we agreed. It turned out to be one of the best experiences the three of us ever had.

When we made the *Little Green Book* video, it was a great feeling to be working with two of the people I loved and respected most. (It was also historic, in a way: It was the first and only time I saw Harvey give Ben a lesson in more than thirty years!) Now the three of us didn't reminisce about old times. The video was purely instructional, but for us it was fabulous.

There was still daylight one day when we finished the parts that were staged, so we lingered on the course and kept talking while the director, Mickey Horrigan, let the cameras run. It was so pleasant and serene out there, the three of us bathed in the last hour of sunlight. Anyone could tell Ben and I were having fun and didn't want to leave.

That night I was expected home to change clothes and take Christy and some guests to dinner. I asked a friend who had been watching the filming to call Christy and say, "Tom's still out with Harvey and Ben. He said that

Harvey and me at the Austin Country Club, where I received the Hickok Professional Athlete Award in February 1993
David Kennedy, *Austin American-Statesman*

it's just too good to stop. You guys go on to dinner and he'll join you later."

Mickey edited the tape and sent us each a copy. He called it "The Jam Session." It shows the three of us talking golf and isn't for sale or public consumption. It was a picture of Harvey doing what he did best with two of his lifelong pupils, who were soaking up every word, loving every minute.

Some time later, in the spring of 1995, steadily the life began to ebb away from this born teacher who was so giving that he had spent most of his ninety years trying to avoid saying "no." It is still difficult for me to shake the picture of Harvey when he was sick and frail and crippled, the battle dragging on in so many parts of his body. It pains me, the thought of him hunched over, fiddling with his hearing aid, trying to make sure the gadget worked so he could hear you. It was so painful for him to turn, that when someone came alongside a minute or so might pass before he recognized them.

There was one more hospital stay, in March, when an ambulance rushed him to St. David's. A paramedic asked a question about his grip. Harvey had pneumonia now and every breath was an effort, but he answered him gladly. That was typical of him.

Three weeks later they let him go home to die. This time his family and his friends knew there would be no beating the clock. He would not get another extension to let him bask in the fame he didn't need, or spend the money he never expected.

He could no longer make the effort to get out of bed. His weight had dropped below ninety pounds the day Ben and Julie brought their two little girls to the house to say good-bye. Ben was leaving to play at New Orleans and tune up his game for the Masters.

Harvey's hearing was just about completely gone and he couldn't make his mouth obey his brain. The sounds he made were mostly mumbles, thick and inaudible. Then the Crenshaws showed up. He knew Ben had been struggling with his short game. I'm not sure how, but he always knew these things.

And then this remarkable transformation took place. As Tinsley told it, Harvey, in a clear, reasonably firm voice, asked Ben to get a putter he kept in the corner and bring it to his bedside. Then he had Ben take a couple of practice strokes on the carpet. Harvey didn't sit bolt upright, but he turned on his side and told Ben to trust himself.

What else he and Ben said to each other after that is part of Ben's story now. He related it after he won the Masters: how he told Harvey he loved him and Harvey replied, "I love you, too, Ben. I will be watching you always."

And Ben fought back the tears and said, "I know you will."

We knew Harvey wouldn't be with us much longer, so Ben and I agreed on a plan. I was scheduled to stay in Austin through Sunday, April 2, for the unveiling of a statue of Mr. Penick and me on the lawn next to the clubhouse of the Austin Country Club. I was to call Ben, whatever the news, whenever it came.

Harvey had intended to be at the ceremony, but clearly he could not. The adjustments in the program had been made. Harvey was hanging on to life, giving us a last lesson about grace and fearlessness.

The sculpture showed Mr. Penick studying my swing,

Don Davis's statue of Harvey Penick studying my swing: It was unveiled on April 2, 1995. Harvey died later that same day.
David Kennedy, *Austin American-Statesman*

as he had a thousand times. Ben wasn't included for a very simple reason. He had helped design the course at Barton Creek and had left to become a member there. Mr. Penick understood and expected nothing less.

When Don Davis, the artist, asked for permission to do the sculpture, he was struck by the similarity of Harvey's and my replies. "I've never done anything," said Harvey, "to deserve being made into a statue." I said, "I've never done anything to deserve being made into a statue beside Mr. Penick."

Harvey's reaction was right in character. Mine was simply the truth. But how could you not feel flattered? Harvey had been a part of the Austin Country Club's history for seventy years. My family had owned a membership since I was thirteen. I would like to think that the Kites had brought the club some favorable publicity. Now we were giving the pigeons a break.

Harvey had his lucid moments, and people came to visit, but the chatter in the house didn't really reach him except at odd times. On the Sunday the statue was to be unveiled, I dropped by his house in the morning with Christy and the twins, David and Paul. Our daughter, Stephanie, was thirteen, old enough to be uneasy when death was close by, and she had gone to a gymnastics meet. In the afternoon, I went to the club for the unveiling ceremony. He had kept himself alive for this occasion, I am almost sure, but there was no longer any realistic chance that he could attend the ceremony.

Tinsley spoke on behalf of his father:

". . . He is with us in spirit, but I think he might be embarrassed by all the fuss and attention. My father has often told me the most important thing that ever happened to him was going to Hyde Park Christian Church one day in 1924 and having his eyes come to rest on a young woman in the choir. Her name was Helen and he likes to say he chased her until he caught her.

"My mother likes to say that 'she chased him' till he caught her.

"The second most important thing that ever happened to him was his eighth birthday. That was when my grandmother allowed him to join his four older brothers as a caddy at Austin Country Club. This was in 1912, the year before Francis Ouimet won the U.S. Open.

"Austin Country Club was located at Red River and Thirty-eighth Street—the course now known as Hancock Municipal. The greens were sand. He always described himself as a lucky man who was privileged to be able to work outdoors, doing something he loved, with friends and people who shared his love for the game.

"My father is especially honored to be featured in this statue with one of his greatest students, Tom Kite. He would tell you that Tommy exemplifies the finest qualities a golfer can have: dedication to his craft, sportsmanship, and abiding love for the spirit of the game.

"Tommy is a role model for all players young and old.

"Don [Davis], you've done a magnificent job. I wish my father's health would have permitted him to be with us out here today . . ."

When it was my turn to speak, I had trouble keeping my voice from cracking. I acknowledged the break I knew I had gotten when my dad moved us to Austin and put me in the custody of the greatest golf teacher of all time.

I returned to the Penick house and went to Harvey's bedside. I held his hand and gave him a full report on

Helen Penick (left) and my mother at the entrance to the Austin Country
Club, in front of the life-sized statue of Harvey giving me a lesson
Courtesy of Tinsley Penick

the unveiling: who was there, what was said, how awe-
some the statue was. As we talked, I could feel him weak-
ening, and then he startled me by asking how Davis Love
III was doing in the tournament at New Orleans. Davis
needed a win to qualify for the Masters. His father, Davis
Love, Jr., who had played college golf under Harvey and
gone on to become a fine teacher, spreading the gospel
according to Penick, had died in a plane crash in 1988.

It was not unusual, I suppose, that at ninety Harvey out-
lived some of his favorite students: Morris Williams, Davis Love, Jr., George Knudson.

I walked into the living room, where a crowd of family
and friends had gathered around the big-screen TV. Davis
was in a play-off for the title. When I went back to the
bedroom and told Harvey that Davis was leading, he
clapped his hands. It was weak and awkward, but a spon-
taneous gesture. Where he got the energy, I can't imagine.

Davis Love won the tournament, and seconds later
Harvey was gone. Harvey's son-in-law, Billy Powell, was
announcing the results as he walked into the bedroom. I
want to believe that Harvey heard him.

It was Knudson, a onetime Canadian PGA champion,
who said, "I really believe that Harvey is the only man
who knows all there is to know about this game. It's
funny how we got together. Davis was the one who
wanted to see him. I was just along for the ride, on my
way to a tournament. I got out of the car with Davis and
Harvey gave me a lesson."

And what a ride it had been for so many of us.

Ben was in Augusta for the Masters by this time.
Around six o'clock I walked out to the deck of the Penick
home and called him on my cell phone. The conversa-
tion wasn't long. We were both choked up, but we reminded each other what a great life Harvey had and how
many people he had touched.

I was scheduled to join Ben in Augusta the next morning. We would play practice rounds Monday and Tuesday, then charter a plane to fly us to the funeral in Austin on Wednesday, along with our wives and Terry Jastrow. Ben and I would both be pallbearers.

We flew back through a storm, and it was raining when we landed in Austin. The crowd spilled outside the funeral home and huddled under umbrellas. At the cemetery, Ben and I helped place the casket over the grave, then laid a flower on top. A tent shielded the mourners from the rain. Bud Shrake gave the eulogy.

The sun broke through on the flight back to Augusta, and one of us probably should have taken that as an omen. What followed was a storybook week when Ben, with an angel on his shoulder, played superb golf to win his second Masters. One of his shots hit a tree and kicked back onto the green. Do you believe in miracles?

Since that week, life has gone on. It always does. Neither Ben nor I won a tournament in 1996 or the first four months of 1997, although I finished second to Tiger Woods in a Masters that all but rewrote the record book—and the history books.

I had no reason to think it would be that long before I'd come close to winning another major tournament. Since my triumph in the 1992 Open I had been playing as well as I had ever played—as well as any other player

After winning the 1993 Los Angeles Open: With the $180,000 prize money, I became the first golfer to exceed $8 million in career winnings.
AP/Wide World Photos

around, I honestly thought. I was riding the momentum of that match, and my confidence was at a peak when I won the L.A. Open on the last day of February 1993.

At Los Angeles, I was four shots behind with seven holes to play. But with five birdies down the stretch, I finished in front by three strokes and passed the eight-million-dollar mark in career winnings. I was still Number 1 on the money list and two-for-three on the season, having walked off with the Bob Hope Desert Classic two weeks earlier. I set a tour record for ninety holes in that one, at 35 under par.

As luck would have it, I was one of those athletes who really did go to Disney World (and I wasn't making a TV commercial). It happened while I was touring Universal Studios in the early summer of 1993. I was horsing around with my kids on one of the rides and felt a pain in my back. As a result I had to pull out of a couple of tournaments and went through weeks of discomfort before the doctors determined that I had two herniated discs.

I recovered pretty much on schedule, but I spent more months trying to rediscover my stroke. It's like disarming a bomb: Being approximately right, getting close, isn't usually good enough.

The fans wanted to be kind, and a bunch of them had commented to me, "You're not playing much, are you?" The truth is I was playing about as much as ever. They just didn't see my name on the leader board.

But those remarks from my fans were just what I needed to motivate me. Going through a slump, you just want to set your jaw and say, Darn it, people say I can't play out here anymore, at forty-five or forty-seven. I say I can. I'm going to show them. And the 1997 Masters felt like a perfect spot to begin a turnaround.

The question of age brings to mind a story Tinsley Penick tells about a wealthy visitor who showed up one day at the Austin Country Club. He had been a championship golfer as a junior and in high school. He was forty-five and had made enough money in business to retire. He wanted to renew his interrupted golf career and fulfill his dream. He wanted to take lessons from Tinsley every day and in five years he would try his luck on the PGA Senior Tour.

Tinsley told him, "By sheer coincidence, we have a member here at the club who is in a similar situation you're in. Like you, he's forty-five. He's made all the money he'll ever need. He has a handsome family. He practices golf every day and in five years he'll be ready for the Senior Tour. He's your competition, the player you are going to have to beat. He's sitting over there," and Tinsley pointed to the dining room, "having a sandwich."

He brought him over to my table and said, "I want you to meet Tom Kite."

I learned later the story behind the introduction. As the incident made the rounds of the club, I got as big a kick out of it as anyone. Still, I must offer a disclaimer.

My thoughts are not on the Senior Tour. I am not thinking about anything that is four years in the future. I don't
believe I am finished winning on the regular PGA tour.

I am thinking about the one thing I have always con-
centrated on: playing well. If you play well, winning will
take care of itself. That's another lesson Harvey impressed upon us.

The lessons Harvey Penick taught his students about
golf and life were lessons that will stay with us always.
To say we miss him would be a serious understatement.
His positive energy, generosity, and good humor made
all the difference in our lives.

Those are just a few of the reasons why he'll always
stay in my memory. His years of suffering, which I've
recounted, are still vivid to me because he was so patient
and brave. But I have many other, lighthearted memories.
I can't condense thirty years into one vignette, but here
are some of my fondest recollections:

I remember him as a meticulous man. The year I met
him, in 1963, he bought a pair of alligator shoes. He
loved those shoes and kept them shined so that you
could see your reflection in them. When he died, he was
buried in those shoes.

I remember him from the putting green. I have a photograph on my wall of Harvey giving me a lesson. His
hands fit the club in a perfect grip.

I remember him with my kids, how he asked them to

In 1995 Harvey Penick was guest of honor at a dinner given by Caritaf of Austin to establish the Harvey Penick Award for Excellence in the Game of Life. Helen Penick is seated next to Harvey; behind are me and Christy, Julie and Ben Crenshaw. Copyright © by Carrell Grigsby

do the backflips they learned in gymnastics whenever they came to his house. How that tickled him.

I remember him sitting on his favorite stool on those cold, rainy days, twirling a golf club as if it were a baton while he talked golf.

I remember how he never lost his sense of humor, even when he was in constant pain, unable to stand erect, walking around hunched over his cane, his spine so curved he looked, as someone observed, like a question mark. "When I was younger," he said, "I used to recognize people by their swings. Now I recognize them by their shoes."

I remember how he always wanted me to be less intense. I'm still working on it. Christy and I have talked about it. Bob Rotella stresses what Mr. Penick urged: Go to the golf course. Don't get hung up on the practice tee.

It occurs to me that I never played a round of golf with Mr. Penick. Ben Crenshaw probably did, but he started out with him a few years before I came along. I would have enjoyed playing with him, but I do not rank it as a regret. I have none concerning Harvey. Oh, I would like to have had the benefit of his wisdom and friendship for a few more years. But I had it for thirty. I can't say that I was short-changed.

I didn't leave anything unsaid, either. I thanked him for making me a player, and a better person, and for teaching me to take dead aim. I loved him and I told him so.

There's very little left to say, except to pay Harvey Penick a final tribute: Those who knew him considered that he was as close to being a saintly man as a golfer can be.

WATER HOLE #6

Entry, September 30, 1955

Most women learn golf from their husbands—or try to learn from them. Husbands invariably tell their better half to "look at the ball" or "keep your head down."

I showed a lady from San Antonio that I can look at the ball and still miss it.

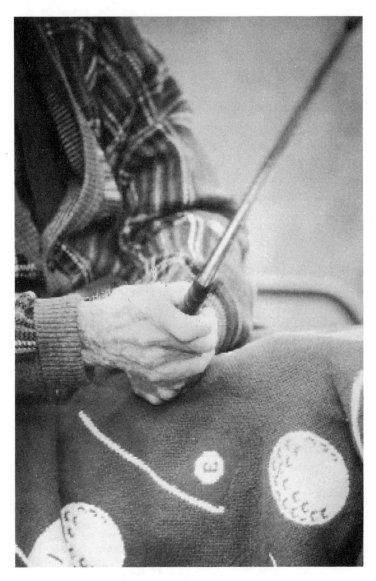

Gary Edwards

Epilogue

I have been twice blessed, at least, in my golf career, to have had Harvey Penick as my coach and to have a father who was also my best friend.

And how important are the moms, like mine, Mauryene Kite, who schlep you to practice and to the tournaments when you're still too young to drive? Christy does it now with our kids.

My dad walks the Masters with me each year, and most of the Texas events I play in. He worries more about my game than I do, and he can spot a flaw just as quickly. When I was slow to snap back from my injury in 1993, he summed up the problem in a sentence: "When you're missing a lot of little putts, it's because your confidence has been bruised."

You don't get to the PGA Tour, much less make it—whatever "making it" means to you—without that kind of support. And I have to say this for Mr. Penick: Our parents are obligated to love us; Harvey volunteered.

When I first decided to undertake this book, Dr. Bob Rotella, a sports psychologist at the University of Virginia, who has advised me many times, urged me to strive for two goals: Tell how Harvey affected my life and tell why my career turned out the way it did. He told me to stress the patience and commitment and hard work it takes to become a top player. I hope I've done so.

You try to cover as many questions as you can, and here are the ones I am most often asked:

Q. Are teachers of Harvey Penick's kind disappearing from the golf scene?

A. Unfortunately, yes. A number of factors are making his type of professional, the all-around club pro, obsolete. With golf becoming more commercial, today's professionals are specializing to the point that they are merchandisers, businessmen, club directors, or teachers—rarely are they all of the above.

You'd think that because a teacher concentrates solely on coaching, he'd become an even better teacher, but in practice he takes on more and more students from all parts of the country, and as a result spends increasingly less time with each student. A great coach based in North Carolina, for example, may see a pro from Dallas or Chicago only a couple times a year at best.

I had access to Mr. Penick every week, but today, even if you live in the same city as a top coach, you won't have that kind of access. Those coaches with a national reputation spend much of the year traveling to lecture at golf schools, give clinics, and keep numerous other commitments.

Q. What is the exact meaning of the phrase "take dead aim"?

A. This was sort of Harvey's Rosetta stone. People can interpret it as they want, use it as they need. In the *Little Red Book*, Harvey recalled sending a telegram to one of his pupils, Betsy Rawls, before a playoff in the women's U.S. Open. Betsy won. The telegram contained that single sentence: "Take dead aim!" Over the years, he did this many times with many golfers.

I can't count how often I left his company with that phrase echoing in my ears, before a college match or after I went on the tour.

Harvey wasn't sure he had explained it fully when he wrote that it meant, "Shut out all thoughts other than picking out a target and taking dead aim at it." So he revisited the subject in his third book, with the blue cover, *The Game for a Lifetime*. Clearly, many of his readers had written or asked him to expand on his thoughts.

"When I ask you to take dead aim," he wrote, "I mean that for a few seconds you should become calm but aware, putting all your best attention to the moment at hand. . . . Your body will do what your mind tells you to

do. You have no doubt, no fear. For those few seconds
you are what you think."

To Bud Shrake, it meant, "You should pay your very
best attention to what you are doing at this moment.
Don't let other outside thoughts interfere, and do it without doubt or fear."

Ben Crenshaw summed it up in two words: "Trust
yourself."

My own definition was, "Clear your mind, focus on
this shot, see it, feel it, picture exactly where you want
it to go. For this moment, you can make time stand still."
This is a discipline you can apply to any task or challenge.

Q. How would you describe Harvey Penick as a
teacher, and did you ever have a disagreement with him?

A. The closest we ever came to disagreeing was when
I tried to convince him, at times, that I needed help. The
best way I can describe him is to say that he was as
comfortable as a pair of old blue jeans, so asking for help
was never hard. He knew you could not treat two golfers
alike or teach them in the same way, and so he liked to
chew on a question, choosing his words with precision
to suit the pupil in question. "The advice you give one
golfer about his pivot might mean an entirely different
thing to a golfer who used to play basketball, or who
had never played any sport," he once observed.

His philosophy about his work was that it should

"guide the learning." When he gave a lesson he never let a student take the blame for any lack of progress and was always quick to say, "It's not your fault that you're not able to hit that fade. I'm just not communicating it right. Let me try to put it another way."

Q. How much jealousy or envy is there on the PGA Tour?

A. Not as much as you might think. Given the number of tournaments and the number of players, you can't expect to win everything—no matter how successful you are. There's no resentment against someone who wins as long as everybody gets what they perceive as their share. Now, if you have a group of players at a certain level and one suddenly emerges as more successful and starts breaking away, the others might find it hard to accept. Take Arnold Palmer, Jack Nicklaus, Lee Trevino, Gary Player, and maybe Tom Watson: They'd risen so high they were in a class by themselves, and few other players could relate to them. My daughter, Stephanie, will face the same situation if she pursues a career as a gymnast. "If you're serious about competing," I've told her, "the higher you climb the ladder, the harder it is to hang on to old friendships. You don't plan it that way, but people go in different directions, and you have to be willing to find new friends."

Q. What do you consider the biggest change in the tour from, say, Hogan's time to now?

A. The lifestyle is totally different. You don't hear much anymore of the Walter Hagen, Jimmy Demaret, Doug Sanders kind of all-night partying, hanging around the piano bar and singing up a storm. In the 1940s and into the early 1950s, the tour was just trying to survive. The players traveled almost like a pack of wolves. A lone wolf doesn't have nearly the possibility of success as a pack does. So in the early stages of the PGA Tour, the guys were dependent on one another. They traveled together, ate and drank together, shared rooms.

At night they gathered in the hotel bar, where the likes of Demaret, Dutch Harrison, Lloyd Mangrum, Porky Oliver, and Sam Snead held court. "What a floor show that was!" said Doug Sanders.

Their times had little in common with mine, but I love the stories they told, the color they brought to the game. For example, as he strolled to the next hole, Sanders would at odd moments quote the poet Kahlil Gibran: "How can you think of yourself as generous if you receive gold and give back silver?" Or he might quote the quaint limericks of an unknown author: "I knew I had him, had him good; he was up to his ass in Johnson grass and Louisiana wood."

Golf was Doug's ticket out of the cotton patch in Cedartown, Georgia. He went on to win twenty tournaments, all the while earning his reputation as a party monster. "I knew my weaknesses," he says, "even though a lot of times I've done nothing about them. I've been up and down, and that's the way I lived my life. It has never been plain vanilla. I'm the guy who got plugged in the back of the head by Spiro Agnew. I'm the guy who lost the British Open on a two-and-a-half-foot putt [to Nicklaus, in 1970]. I've enjoyed all of it. I wouldn't turn the clock back one tick."

Q. What about the galleries you draw on the tour today? Have they changed, too?

A. The crowds are getting younger, more diverse, in some ways less educated about the finer points of the game. Gone are the days when a golfer would shank a shot and blame it on hearing the click of a camera or the flutter of a butterfly. We accept the fact that some of the fans are noisier and use their lungs, not polite applause, to show their approval. I didn't know what to think the first time I heard a couple of guys yell out, "You the man! You the man!" It isn't a bad thing to let the fans get involved. They want to express themselves in a more intimate way, as they do at baseball or football games. Where I draw the line is if they try to do the wave.

Q. Given the greater stakes, and the growing number of good players, has life on the tour gotten less mannered and civil?

A. To me, the character of the players remains remarkably high. When John Daly admitted he had a drinking problem, it was as close to a moral crisis as anyone could remember. You simply don't have the drugs, sex, or gunplay that have haunted our major team sports. Golf is the only sport where the players truly observe an honor system. And I am not referring to the kind that we recently identified with the Dallas Cowboys: "Yes, your honor. No, your honor."

At least two elements make golf a game of distinction. As Sam Snead once said in an argument with one of baseball's great hitters, "We have to play our foul balls." And we call our own penalties.

If this was not a game of honor, I probably would have two more titles on my list. In 1978, at Pinehurst, North Carolina, I called a penalty stroke on myself when my ball moved. Nobody else saw it, but that didn't matter. It had no bearing on my obligation. I saw the ball move and never considered not calling the penalty. I wasn't a martyr, just a guy observing the code. Ultimately, I lost the tournament, at a time when I had only one win and was aching for another. A week later, I won the British Columbia Open. At the end of the year, the USGA awarded me the Bob Jones Award for "distinguished sportsmanship," certainly worth at least one championship.

In 1993, I was leading the Kemper Open and was paired with Grant Waite of New Zealand. Near the fourth green, he took a drop from a "ground under repair" area. As he prepared to hit to the green, I noticed his heel was still inside the marker. I pointed out his footing to Grant and, yes, he saved what would have been a two-stroke penalty. He went on to win the tourney by one shot. I finished second.

I told Mr. Penick later, "I thought it would be pretty chicken for me to stand by and watch a guy accidentally break a rule and then say, 'By the way, add two strokes.' That's not golf. That's other sports where guys are trying to get every advantage they can get."

Harvey said he was prouder of that gesture than he was of my winning the U.S. Open. That compliment was reward enough.

Q. What does the future hold for you and Ben Crenshaw?

A. Ben will continue to design courses, and I believe he will become one of the premier golf architects in the country. I think Ben has reached a point where he actually enjoys that work more than playing.

I enjoy looking at the raw land and imagining a golf course, but not nearly as much as I still enjoy playing. There is nothing that excites me more than the competition. True, there is competition in other endeavors, including the design business, but it isn't the last-man-standing type of emotion you get on the course.

The good news is that in both our cases, we came along at a time when the money on the PGA Tour was really good. (Since 1990, the total purses have grown 39 percent, or $15.4 million.) We both have been well advised and very fortunate in handling our money. Neither of us made any killer investments. Basically, we can go in any direction we want. If Ben wants to stick to designing, he will. If I want to play, for as long as I can, then let me play.

Whatever we do, we both have a feeling Harvey will be watching us.

Tom Kite's Career Highlights

PGA TOUR RECORD

EXEMPT STATUS: Winner, 1992 U.S. Open
FULL NAME: Thomas Oliver Kite, Jr.
HEIGHT: 5' 8"   **WEIGHT:** 163
BIRTHDATE: December 9, 1949   **BIRTHPLACE:** McKinney, TX
RESIDENCE: Austin, TX
FAMILY: Wife, Christy; Stephanie Lee (10/7/81), David Thomas and Paul
      Christopher (9/1/84)
COLLEGE: University of Texas   **SPECIAL INTERESTS:** Landscaping
TURNED PROFESSIONAL: 1972   **Q SCHOOL:** Fall 1972

TOUR VICTORIES (19): 1976 IVB-Bicentennial Golf Classic. **1978** B.C. Open.
1981 American Motors-Inverrary Classic. **1982** Bay Hill Classic. **1983** Bing
Crosby National Pro-Am. **1984** Doral-Eastern Open, Georgia-Pacific Atlanta Classic. **1985** MONY Tournament of Champions. **1986** Western Open. **1987** Kemper Open. **1989** Nestle Invitational, THE PLAYERS Championship, Nabisco
Championships. **1990** Federal Express St. Jude Classic. **1991** Infiniti Tournament
of Champions. **1992** BellSouth Classic, U.S. Open. **1993** Bob Hope Chrysler
Classic, Nissan Los Angeles Open.

INTERNATIONAL VICTORIES (3): 1974 Air New Zealand Open (Australia). **1980** European Open (Europe). **1996** Oki Pro-Am (Spain).

BEST 1996 FINISH: 2—Canon Greater Hartford Open.

1996 SEASON: 1997 U.S. Ryder Cup Captain saw moments of sunshine and
improvement in 1996 . . . nearly doubled the money he earned in 1995, when he fell
to 104th on money list from 22nd the year before . . . brightest week came at the
Canon Greater Hartford Open . . . bounced back from opening 72 to shoot 68-66-

68 and finish second, four strokes behind D.A. Weibring . . . trailed by three after 54 holes . . . the $162,000 paycheck, his biggest of the year, was almost as much as he won in all of 1995 ($178,580) . . . had three top-15 finishes prior to Hartford: T13 at Bob Hope Chrysler Classic, T11 at Greater Greensboro Chrysler Classic, and T14 at Shell Houston Open . . . headed into end of 1996 with "some positive feelings about my game," thanks to win at OKI Pro-Am in Madrid, Spain . . . victory was his first tournament win since 1993 Nissan Los Angeles Open . . . birdied final hole at La Moraleja GC to edge Argentina's Angel Cabrera by one stroke and earn $117,000 . . . two weeks later, joined Jay Haas to capture Franklin Templeton Shark Shootout, for which each received $150,000.

CAREER HIGHLIGHTS: Biggest victory came in 1992 U.S. Open at Pebble Beach, where even-par 72 in tough Sunday conditions gave him two-stroke win over Jeff Sluman . . . victory earlier that year at BellSouth Classic ended 16-month victory drought . . . made 21 of 25 cuts in 1995, but had only one top-10 finish, T7 at Northern Telecom Open . . . relinquished top position on career money list to Greg Norman after 1995 NEC World Series of Golf . . . got off to blazing start in 1993, posting two wins, a second and eighth in five starts before a March back injury slowed him . . . was untouchable in 1993 Bob Hope Chrysler Classic, closing with rounds of 64-65-62 to set TOUR record for most strokes under par in 90-hole event . . . finished at 35-under 325, which also was good for six-stroke win over Rick Fehr . . . in next start, Nissan Los Angeles Open, even weather couldn't stop him . . . 4-under-par 67 on final day of rain-shortened event produced 19th career victory . . . owns two Arnold Palmer Awards as TOUR's leading money-winner: in 1981, when he made $375,699, and 1989, when he earned more than $1 million more ($1,395,278) . . . THE PLAYERS Championship one of three victory highlights of million-dollar campaign, which culminated in win at season-ending Nabisco Championships . . . 1981 GWAA Player of Year . . . 1989 PGA Player of Year . . . winner 1979 Bob Jones award . . . Rookie of Year for 1973 . . . winner 1981-82 Vardon trophies . . . co-winner with Ben Crenshaw of 1972 NCAA Championship . . . won 1981 JCPenny Classic (with Beth Daniel) and 1992 Shark Shootout (with Davis Love III), to go along with 1996 victory with Jay Haas.

PERSONAL: Three of last four TOUR victories came on holidays: BellSouth Classic (Mother's Day), U.S. Open (Father's Day), Bob Hope Chrysler Classic (Valentine's Day) . . . serves as spokesman for Chrysler Junior Golf Scholarship program . . . started playing golf at six, won first tournament at 11.

PGA TOUR CAREER SUMMARY   PLAYOFF RECORD: 6–4

YEAR	EVENTS PLAYED	CUTS MADE	1ST	2ND	3RD	TOP 10	TOP 25	EARNINGS	RANK
1971 (AM.)	1	1							
1972 (AM.)	4	4					2		
1972	2	2						$2,582	202
1973	34	32				3	16	$54,270	52
1974	28	27			1	8	18	$82,055	25
1975	26	21		1	1	9	14	$87,046	18
1976	27	25	1			8	15	$116,181	20
1977	29	27		1	3	7	16	$125,204	14
1978	28	25	1	1	3	8	15	$161,370	11
1979	28	24			3	11	15	$166,878	17
1980	26	22		1		10	18	$152,490	20
1981	26	26	1	3	3	21	24	$375,699	1
1982	25	24	1	4	1	15	17	$341,081	3
1983	25	21	1	2		8	16	$257,066	9
1984	25	21	2	1		10	14	$348,640	5
1985	24	21	1	1	1	6	11	$258,793	14
1986	26	24	1	1	1	9	13	$394,164	7
1987	24	21	1	2		11	18	$525,516	8
1988	25	21		3	1	10	16	$760,405	5
1989	23	23	3	1		10	14	$1,395,278	1
1990	22	21	1		1	9	15	$658,202	15
1991	25	19	1	1	1	4	9	$396,580	39
1992	23	22	2	1	1	9	17	$957,445	6
1993	20	14	2	2		8	10	$887,811	8
1994	23	18		1	1	8	12	$658,689	22
1995	25	21				1	4	$178,580	104
1996	21	15		1		1	5	$319,326	66
Total	616	542	19	28	22	204	344	$9,661,354	2

1997 PGA TOUR CHARITY TEAM: Tucson Chrysler Classic

TOP TOURNAMENT SUMMARY

Year	71	72	74	75	76	77	78	79	80	81	82	83	84	85	86
Masters Tournament	T42	T27		T10	T5	T3	T18	5	T6	T5	T5	T2	T6	CUT	T2
U.S. Open		T19	T8			T27	T20		CUT	T20	29	T20	CUT	13	T35
British Open Championship				T5			T2	T30	T27		CUT	T29	T22	T8	CUT
PGA Championship			T39	T33	T13	T13		T35	T20	T4	T9	T67	T34	T12	T26
THE PLAYERS Championship			T19	T40	T17		T28	T9	T31	DNS	T27	T27	T51	T64	T4

TOP TOURNAMENT SUMMARY (CONT.)

Year	87	88	89	90	91	92	93	94	95	96
Masters Tournament	T24	44	T18	T14	56		CUT	4	CUT	CUT
U.S. Open	T46	T36	T9	T56	T37	1	CUT	T33	T67	T82
British Open Championship	T72	T20	T19	CUT	T44	T19	T14	T8	T58	T26
PGA Championship	T10	T4	T34	T40	T52	T21	T56	T9	T54	CUT
THE PLAYERS Championship	T9	T11	1	T5	CUT	T35	CUT	T9	T43	CUT
THE TOUR Championship	T17	2	1	18		T13	T7	T22		

NATIONAL TEAMS: Walker Cup, 1971; Ryder Cup (7), 1979, 1981, 1983, 1985, 1987, 1989, 1993; Ryder Cup Captain 1997; U.S. vs. Japan (3), 1982, 1983, 1984; World Cup (2), 1984, 1985; Kirin Cup, 1987 (medalist); Dunhill Cup (4), 1989, 1990, 1992, 1994; Asahi Glass Four Tours, 1989

1996 PGA TOUR STATISTICS

Scoring	70.73	(48)
Driving	259.7	(153)
Driving Accuracy	70.5	(64)
Total Driving	217	(136)
Greens in Regulation	67.4	(56T)
Putting	1.810	(143T)
Sand Saves	51.7	(109T)
Eagles	242.0	(183)
Birdies	3.39	(91T)
All Around	847	(119)

MISCELLANEOUS STATISTICS

Scoring Average Before Cut	71.40	(103T)
Scoring Average 3rd Round	70.43	(55)
Scoring Average Final Round	71.73	(134)
Birdies Conversion %	27.7	(118T)
Par Breakers	18.9	(107T)

1996 Low Round: 66: 4 times, most recent 1996 Buick Open/3
Career Low Round: 62: 4 times, most recent 1993 Bob Hope Chrysler Classic/5
Career Largest Paycheck: $450,000: 1989 Nabisco Championship/1

RYDER CUP TEAMS

1979   Andy Bean, Lee Elder, Hubert Green, Mark Hayes, Hale Irwin, Tom Kite, John Mahaffey, Gil Morgan, Larry Nelson, Lee Trevino, Lanny Wadkins, Fuzzy Zoeller. Captain: Billy Caspar. Results: U.S.A. 17, Europe 11.

1981   Ben Crenshaw, Ray Floyd, Hale Irwin, Tom Kite, Bruce Lietzke, Johnny Miller, Larry Nelson, Jack Nicklaus, Jerry Pate, Bill Rogers, Lee Trevino, Tom Watson. Captain: Dave Marr. Results: U.S.A. 181/2, Europe 91/2.

1983   Ben Crenshaw, Ray Floyd, Bob Gilder, Jay Haas, Tom Kite, Gil Morgan, Calvin Peete, Craig Stadler, Curtis Strange, Lanny Wadkins, Tom Watson, Fuzzy Zoeller. Captain: Jack Nicklaus. Results: U.S.A. 141/2, Europe 131/2.

1985   Ray Floyd, Hubert Green, Peter Jacobsen, Tom Kite, Andy North, Calvin Peete, Mark O'Meara, Craig Stadler, Curtis Strange, Lanny Wadkins, Fuzzy Zoeller. Captain: Lee Trevino. Results: Europe 161/2, U.S.A. 111/2.

1987   Andy Bean, Mark Calcavecchia, Ben Crenshaw, Tom Kite, Larry Mize, Larry Nelson, Dan Pohl, Scott Simpson, Payne Stewart, Curtis Strange, Hal Sutton, Lanny Wadkins. Captain: Jack Nicklaus. Results: Europe 15, U.S.A. 13.

1989   Paul Azinger, Chip Beck, Mark Calcavecchia, Fred Couples, Ken Green, Tom Kite, Mark McCumber, Mark O'Meara, Payne Stewart, Curtis Strange, Lanny Wadkins, Tom Watson. Captain: Raymond Floyd. Results: Europe 14, U.S.A. 14.

1993   Paul Azinger, Chip Beck, John Cook, Fred Couples, Raymond Floyd, Jim Gallagher, Jr., Lee Janzen, Tom Kite, Davis Love III, Corey Pavin, Payne Stewart, Lanny Wadkins. Captain: Tom Watson. Results: U.S.A. 15, Europe 13.

Tom Kite's Recommended Reading List

Jones, Bobby. *Bobby Jones on Golf: The Classic Instructional by Golf's Greatest Legend.* New York: Doubleday & Company, Inc., 1992.

Kite, Tom. *How to Play Consistent Golf.* New York: Pocket Books, 1990.

Penick, Harvey, with Bud Shrake. *And If You Play Golf, You're My Friend.* New York: Simon & Schuster, 1993.

————. *The Game for a Lifetime.* New York: Simon & Schuster, 1996.

————. *Harvey Penick's Little Red Book: Lessons and Teachings from a Lifetime of Golf.* New York: Simon & Schuster, 1992.

Official Media Guide. Ponte Verda Beach, Fla.: PGA Tour Creative Services, 1997.

PGA of America. *Media Guide.* Palm Beach Gardens, Fla., 1997.

MAGAZINES, NEWSPAPERS, NEWS SERVICES, AND OTHER SOURCES

Associated Press (Bob Green, writer)

Austin American-Statesman (Del Lemon, John Maher, Mark Rosner, writers)

Dallas Morning News (Blackie Sherrod, David Casstevens, writers)

Golf Digest (Dan Jenkins, Mickey Herskowitz, writers)

Houston Chronicle (Jayne Custred, John Lopez, writers)

Knight-Ridder Newspapers (Bill Lyon, writer)

Los Angeles Times (Mal Florence, Thomas Bonk, writers)

Sports Illustrated (Dan Jenkins, John Garrity, writers)

USA TODAY (Steve Hershey, writer)